Well
being

Emma Woolf

Wellbeing

Body confidence,
health and happiness

sheldon PRESS

First published in Great Britain in 2019

Sheldon Press
36 Causton Street
London SW1P 4ST
www.sheldonpress.co.uk

British Library Cataloguing-in-Publication Data
A catalogue record for this book is available from the British Library

ISBN 978-1-84709-477-3
eBook ISBN 978-1-84709-478-0

Typeset by Fakenham Prepress Solutions, Fakenham, Norfolk NR21 8NL
First printed in Great Britain by Ashford Colour Press
Subsequently digitally printed in Great Britain

eBook by Fakenham Prepress Solutions, Fakenham, Norfolk NR21 8NL

Produced on paper from sustainable forests

To Xander

Contents

About the author

Emma Woolf is a writer, columnist for *The Times* and *Newsweek*, and co-presenter on Channel 4's *Supersize vs Superskinny*. Having studied English at Oxford University, she worked in psychology publishing before going freelance and now writes for a range of newspapers and magazines, and speaks in the UK and internationally. Emma is an arts critic on Radio 4's *Saturday Review*, and a reviewer on BBC Radio 5 Live and BBC London. Other media appearances include *Newsnight*, *Woman's Hour* and *BBC Daily Politics*.

Her first book, *An Apple a Day: A memoir of love and recovery from anorexia*, has been translated around the world. Other non-fiction titles include *The Ministry of Thin*, *Letting Go*, *Positively Primal* and *The A to Z of Eating Disorders*, as well as several novels.

Visit www.emmawoolf.com or Twitter @EJWoolf

Introduction

'The unhappiest generation in a decade', 'stressed', 'anxious' and 'hopeless' – these are just some of the terms that have recently been used to describe young people in the UK. In the past few years, countless studies have reported that depression, anxiety and loneliness are on the increase, as are eating disorders and other self-harming behaviours. Prescriptions for antidepressants are at an all-time high. Levels of happiness and confidence are at an all-time low.

Are things really this bad? And, if so, why? We are more connected than ever before – or so we're told – so why are we feeling so disconnected and depressed? With increasing prosperity and higher educational and living standards, we should be more not less happy, shouldn't we? What's going wrong?

Is it all down to social media – can we just blame it on the internet? Is it the pressure to be perfect, self-criticism and fear of failure? Is the compare-and-despair syndrome online fuelling unrealistic expectations and turning us into nervous wrecks? Or is it simply due to better awareness of mental health issues and reduced stigma around discussing mental illness – and therefore a good sign that it's all out in the open?

The reasons, of course, are multifactorial and it is impossible to generalize about triggers, symptoms, duration or cures. It is gradually being recognized, however, that mental wellbeing is as important as physical wellbeing. We all have the right to a healthy, happy head.

Defining wellbeing

What do we mean when we talk about 'wellbeing'? What does it feel like, what does it look like? 'Wellbeing' clearly signifies more than just 'being well' or not being ill, but the exact meaning can be hard to pin down.

#Wellness is a super-fashionable concept, trending all over social media, but the term 'wellbeing' has been around far longer than you might think. It originally derives from the Old English words 'weal', meaning 'wealth, welfare and wellbeing', and 'wel', meaning 'in a state of good fortune or happiness'. 'Wellbeing' was often used in the collective sense and, indeed, still is – politicians frequently refer to public welfare, doctors refer to the wellbeing of their patients – and, as we have seen, it encompasses prosperity and wealth too. They may be centuries old, but these ancient ideas still capture the essence of what wellbeing means to us today.

Moving into the modern era, two pioneering thinkers in the USA really transformed the concept of wellness. In the 1970s, Don Ardell and John Travis began to challenge the traditional medical model, whereby an individual is considered 'well' if no symptoms of illness are present. Instead, they focused on the importance of self-responsibility, connection and wellness of the body, mind, emotions and spirit. Travis described wellness as 'the loving acceptance of yourself'. Ardell identified 'reason, exuberance, athleticism and liberty' as essential components of total body wellbeing. This was the true birth of the modern wellness revolution.

A few decades on and the terms 'wellbeing' and 'wellness' are back in popular usage, sparking a whole new transformation in how we think about, talk about and treat our physical and mental health. Notions and concepts of wellbeing are casually bandied around by everyone from personal trainers to YouTube vloggers to unqualified celebrity diet gurus. Because of this, wellbeing and wellness are sometimes conflated with the clean eating movement and faddy dieting crazes or are dismissed as empty or meaningless. In fact, with the rising levels of depression and anxiety disorders, the true wellbeing model, in which we strive for optimum physical, emotional and mental health, remains as important as ever.

To me the term 'wellbeing' captures a feeling of being truly comfortable in your own skin. Wellbeing does not need to be fashionable, super-fit or photogenic, and it is probably not something you can share on Instagram or vlog about. It's just a quiet sense of contentment, being at ease in and with your body and peaceful in your mind. This may sound simple but in modern life it is increasingly hard to find.

Why is inner wellness so elusive? Why is personal contentment so fleeting? Why is this holistic, happy equilibrium of mind and body so difficult to hang on to? It depends on more than just eating healthily and exercising regularly, doing well academically or in your career or knowing you have cash in the bank. It's a delicate balance of the mind and body, thoughts, feelings, emotions, brain, head and heart.

Our wellbeing is affected by the people around us, the important relationships in our lives and our physical environment. These days we live such hyperconnected, fast-paced lives that we often underestimate the importance of the world around us. We travel on dirty, crowded trains, live in tower blocks or work in high-rise glass and steel offices, then wonder why we get stressed or anxious. But setting, ambience and the natural world really matter when it comes to finding mental and physical calm. After all, it's hard to feel at peace in a war zone, whether actual or emotional.

The physical and the mental aspects of health have long been divided and treated as separate things. For decades in the UK we have accepted that the National Health Service (NHS) deals with our physical ailments, leaving it to counsellors, therapists or charities to deal with any mental illness. There are signs of progress, however. In 2018, the Prime Minister appointed the first ever Minister for Suicide Prevention, with the aim of reducing the number of suicides and addressing the stigma that stops people seeking help. There is also a growing acceptance that mental and physical health are inextricably linked: recent governments have talked of 'parity of esteem'. In essence this means according the same respect and priority to patients' heads (their mental wellbeing) as they do to their bodies.

When you think about it, this makes sense. If you are diagnosed with a life-changing or terminal illness, it's highly unlikely that this will have no impact on your mood and feelings. For example, depression and insomnia are common side effects in individuals being treated for cancer, yet they cannot be dealt with by the oncology team treating the disease. And so it is with any serious health issue: of course it affects our mental as much as our physical health. We need both physical and mental good health to be truly in a state of wellbeing. What is the benefit of being physically healthy if your mind is unsettled? Or vice versa: how likely are you to find mental peace if you are wracked with physical illness?

Getting to grips with what we expect from our health providers is part of working out what genuine wellbeing means to us as individuals. We cannot expect doctors to fix our broken hearts, but we can and should be able to ask for help with our mental health during tough times.

For too long, mental illness has been misunderstood, overlooked and even hidden. Traditionally, mental 'problems' have been surrounded by shame and guilt and shrouded in secrecy. This is changing, along with the public health changes outlined above, but there is still more work to be done. The more we talk about mental health in balance with and as important (if not more so) as our physical health, the more we reduce the lingering stigma that sufferers might feel.

The truth is that mental illness, whether mild or severe, is not unusual. According to the leading mental health charity in the UK, Mind, approximately 1 in 4 people in the UK will experience a mental health problem each year. Many 'normal' people struggle with conditions such as depression, anxiety or panic disorders, eating disorders, obsessive-compulsive disorder (OCD), bipolar disorder or schizophrenia. Many who are outwardly functioning are dealing with these conditions on a daily basis. The symptoms, including changes in mood, personality and personal habits and social withdrawal, are not always obvious to outsiders, but they can have a serious impact on the individual's life.

Why does mental illness feel so lonely? Emotional distress, worry, despair, obsessions, compulsions and feelings of being unable to cope are far more common than we might think. Yet when we're experiencing difficulties, it can feel like we're all alone. It seems as though the rest of the world is 'sorted' and you are the only one struggling. Our problems can isolate us, making us feel ashamed or abnormal. That statistic of 1 in 4 is a powerful reminder that, whatever is going on inside your head, you are *not* alone. Throughout this book I will be sharing case studies from other readers to remind you of that fact.

Terms such as 'normal' and 'abnormal' are not particularly helpful in the context of mental health. Whatever we are going through feels incredibly real – as the saying goes, *if it matters, it matters*. Nevertheless we must try, where possible, to distinguish between everyday ups and downs and actual mental illness. We must try to be realistic about our own (and society's) unrealistic expectations of happiness. It really is normal to experience life's upsets, periods of low mood, sadness or anxiety. Almost every one of us growing up will face heartache and romantic rejection, disappointment, exam or work stress, insecurity, worry or self-doubt. Every one of us will face loss, bereavement and grief. These experiences are part of the unique pain and privilege of being human. Our emotional scars are signs of strength, not weakness. Surviving the lowest points in life is something to be proud of – even to celebrate – and makes the high points all the more precious. There will be bumps in the road and that is when our true character is tested. We want to be in control, but we're not.

These painful times are also a reminder that it is OK to be sad. Sometimes we simply have to sit with the loneliness. Sometimes we should allow ourselves to cry. And always we should surround ourselves with good friends – and if possible, some good wine or chocolate too. (Of course, if low mood becomes prolonged or anxiety feels unmanageable, you should seek professional help.)

We will delve into these and many other aspects of mental and physical health in this book, exploring their impact on our overall state of wellbeing. Topics include body image, self-esteem and personal confidence, social media, food, nutrition and dieting, disordered eating, helpful and unhelpful influences in recovery, exercise and self-care, relationships, family and friends, coping strategies and much more.

What wellbeing means to others

Before we start, let's look at what wellbeing means to others and at some of the challenges they face in their everyday lives.

❛ *"Wellbeing" means happiness, the ability to live day to day as fully as possible in whatever ways matter to you, sustain you and make you feel most alive. Personally I don't "have it" but it's a work in progress and I still hold the hope that maybe one day I will get there (whatever my "there" might look like).* ❜ **Yasmin, 24**

❛ *To me, "wellbeing" means an all-round sense of health and happiness. It means success in my career and being physically and mentally fit and healthy. It means strong relationships with friends and family and living life to its fullest. On one hand, I no longer have a career due to my mental health – however, there are days when I'd say I feel in "perfect equilibrium". On the other hand, there are days when I feel an absolute mess! . . . I go through phases. Recently I've felt like I've regained the old me, when I look back and realize I've been happy, organizing events and seeing friends – generally being the life and soul and creating memories – I feel like that is the real Karen. But we lose her quite easily to anxiety/depression/stress. I bottled emotions and thoughts up for a long time before completely breaking down and opening up. I think I'm getting better at maintaining me rather than allowing my mental health to isolate and destroy me.* ❜ **Karen, 30**

❛ *The way I see it, "wellbeing" means a healthy state of mind and body – not perfect, but healthy enough to perform daily tasks without hindrance. I do not have that state of wellbeing due to health problems such as severe anaemia, anxiety and depression. I would like to achieve it one day, though.* **Rue, 19**

I think "wellbeing" means understanding what one needs to feel in control of oneself and to find relative contentment in the day-to-day. So, for example, I know that cycling rather than getting public transport, seeing friends, knitting, drinking good wine and doing a job with purpose all contribute to me "being well". I make decisions in my life that prioritize these as I know what a difference they make. I think that wellbeing is different from happiness as wellbeing can help one cope with unhappiness, with uncertainty, without the wheels falling off, so to speak. **Letty, 29**

To me, "wellbeing" is a state of tranquillity. It is getting up in the morning and feeling safe in my surroundings. It is having my mind, body and spirit generally at ease. **Taylor, 19**

To me, "wellbeing" is made up of three categories: physical, mental and emotional. Physical pertains to health, safety and basic needs; mental to psychological and intellectual elements; and emotional to one's contentment, happiness and fulfilment. Personally, I don't think anyone is in perfect equilibrium, there is always room to grow, develop and improve, and "wellbeing" is a lifelong pursuit. I don't believe I have reached ideal wellbeing, nor do I think I ever will. I'm currently in a transitional period, looking for a job and living with my parents. I am lacking the social interaction and sense of achievement that would bring me happiness and fulfilment. **Rachel, 28**

To me, "wellbeing" means being able to get through the day without wanting to go into hiding. To get through feeling comfortable and looking forward to the day ahead. Just generally feeling "well". **Gemma, 21**

For me, a normal level of "wellbeing" is taking care and acknowledging the importance of your physical and mental health while avoiding becoming obsessed with how you "should" feel or how you "should" be taking care of yourself. At this stage in my life I'm certainly aware of the importance of my own wellbeing, yet I do not actively prioritize it, despite knowing that I need to. **Niamh, 18**

Wellbeing means slightly different things to each of us at different times in our lives, but it is clear from these comments that we all recognize what it feels like. Sometimes we take wellbeing for granted, sometimes we put it at risk or don't bother to take care of ourselves. Sometimes we create health problems for ourselves by drinking or smoking, eating too much or too little, exercising excessively or not at all. Sometimes we fail to take warning signs such as stress or burnout seriously, and sometimes life just hits us and we get in a mess.

But change is always possible, no matter how bad things seem. Anxiety, depression or loneliness are not for ever. All of us can do something today to improve our physical and mental health. Acknowledging that your wellbeing matters – and being brave enough to explore it – is a good place to start. And deciding to take your own health and happiness seriously is a fantastic first step.

Body image and wellbeing

A healthy body image is fundamental to physical and mental wellbeing, but what does that actually mean?

'Body image' sounds straightforward, but its true meaning is surprisingly elusive. It involves our bodies, of course, but it's more than that. It's about how we see ourselves in our minds as we move through the world, and not just the physical being we see in the mirror. Body image is at our core – a deeply personal patchwork of how we see ourselves, how we treat ourselves and how we value ourselves. It dictates how we behave and relate to others; it is the foundation on which we build our personality and shape our individual style; it controls the opportunities and ambitions we pursue or don't pursue.

Body image is also a result of our individual experiences in life, our families and our past. In childhood, did your parents talk about bodies with openness or shame? Their attitudes and behaviour during your early years may have influenced whether you grew up feeling physically confident or inadequate. Our schooldays matter too – for example, whether we were sporty or the last one to be picked for the team – and then in adolescence, our first relationships with members of the opposite (or same) sex. At a more serious level, experiences of neglect or sexual abuse in childhood can also have a profound impact on one's lifelong body image.

Seemingly trivial factors affect our body image too. Minor things such as clothes influence how we project ourselves outwardly and feel inwardly. Have you ever worn something too tight or revealing or something that is simply not 'you' and, as a consequence, felt ill at ease with yourself all day? They say that 'clothes maketh the man' (or woman), and the way we present ourselves to the world certainly contributes to our physical self-confidence. Maybe you agreed to try a new hairstyle in a hairdressers and then regretted it for weeks afterwards. Comments or glances from others, the people you're with, the media images you see, even bad lighting in a changing room – these all affect how you feel about your body on any given day.

But body image isn't just about bodies. It is the starting point for how we relate to ourselves and the world around us. Nor is body image fixed or static. It changes from day to day, year to year and often fluctuates at different stages of our lives. We all know happy, physically confident children who have gone on to struggle with body image in adolescence. Life events continue to affect our self-image even after the major body changes of puberty. Episodes of weight gain or pregnancy, for example, may affect our body image negatively, for obvious reasons. Depression, anxiety and other mood disorders can also have a detrimental effect.

Body image covers a wide range of thoughts, feelings and attitudes, but for most of us it will include the:

- **way we visualize our body** not simply the reflection in the mirror but also the mental picture we carry of how we appear to the outside world;
- **language we use about our own body** ask yourself, 'Is it critical?', 'Is it kind?';
- **way we respond to our body's essential needs** such as food and exercise;
- **way we respond to our body during illness or pain**;
- **self-care** listening to our body's other needs, for rest, warmth, pampering, even hugs.

It is already clear from this that 'body image' means a lot more than just what we see when we look in the mirror.

'When I get the perfect body . . .'

Having a negative body image is simply a response to our physical flaws, isn't it? If we're overweight or have bad skin, it's logical that we feel down on ourselves. If we were perfect, we'd be happy, right?

Wrong. Having the 'perfect' body will not give you a healthy body image if you don't feel it inside. As many models and athletes will admit, their apparent physical 'perfection' is not always reflected in their mental wellbeing. They will often talk of the pressure and anxiety associated with achieving and maintaining the ideal body. Many attractive individuals are wracked with insecurity and self-doubt. They fixate on their flaws as much as you or me; they compare up not down, measuring themselves against others whom they perceive to be more beautiful than them. We may long to be as slim or as stunning as them, while secretly they are hating themselves.

You may have discovered this paradox in your own life: being super-thin or ultra-fit does not always correlate with your best-ever body image. For me, and I know that many other women feel the same, some of the most miserable years of my life were spent when I was at my thinnest.

Rather, healthy body image is a combination of emotional and physical input, a complex mix of resilience and optimism, enjoyment in life, nutritious food, good relationships and many other factors that are unique to every individual.

Think of a few people you know, male and female, of different body shapes and sizes. Who seems to be the happiest and most at peace with themselves?

They will probably not be those who are closest to having the 'perfect' body, but the ones who have the most positive attitude towards themselves and others. Instead of measuring themselves against society's unrealistic expectations of perfection or endlessly striving to be a different weight or shape, they have reached a place of self-acceptance and appreciation of their own bodies.

Change your perspective

Here's a quick thought experiment to get you thinking in a different way. Take a moment to think about your body in the following ways.

- **Think of it as a house** Visualize your body as the house in which you live. Do you make it cosy, do you look after it and maintain it, do you fix the roof and gutters when they leak, do you consult experts when things go wrong? Do you keep it warm? Do you occasionally buy nice things for it? Do you keep your house looking smart inside and out and are you proud of it?
- **Think of it as a car** Visualize your body as a well-tuned machine. Would you turn on the engine without putting petrol in first; would you try to make it run on empty? Whether you're imagining an expensive Jaguar or a little Fiat, you wouldn't expect it to function without proper fuel.
- **Think of it as a friend** Take an imaginative leap outside your body and imagine it's the body of a good friend. Would you be critical of the flaws, wobbly bits and so-called imperfections? Would you use harsh language to describe your friends' bodies or repeatedly tell them they were fat or ugly? Would those physical imperfections make you like your friends any less; would you even care?

Your body is your dwelling place for the rest of your life. You wouldn't neglect your house or your car. You wouldn't verbally abuse a good friend or judge him or her by appearance. Sometimes it helps to take a fresh look at body image, to understand why it matters. Yes, the way you think about your body really matters. It is a sort of obligation to maintain the most important machinery you own, the precious place in which you live. It's a relationship with yourself and it requires kindness and self-compassion.

Of course, it's not that simple. In our modern hypervisual, highly judgemental modern culture, it is all too easy to get sucked into the compare-and-despair syndrome. Sadly, having a negative body image is common. These days it is normal to feel critical about your appearance (and abnormal to like your own body). That's why taking an objective stance, thinking of your body in a different way – as a house, a car or a friend – can help.

Mixed messages

What makes body image even more complicated is that we are receiving mixed messages all the time. Confidence is good, but not too much. Be ambitious, but don't be pushy. Be assertive, but not aggressive. Is it any wonder we get confused?

It starts early. Most girls and young women grow up with contra-dictory guidance on how they should look and behave. We are told that girls can be as clever as boys, that we should strive to get high grades and make it to the top of our chosen career, but we are also constantly reminded to dress a certain way, wear the right make-up, stay fit and, above all, slim. The media and wider society bombard young women with an avalanche of different advice; we should be physically confident no matter what we look like, but we should also conform to a certain look. Magazines that tell us to 'love our bodies' also body-shame female celebrities. They vilify women for gaining or losing too much weight, zooming in on beach photos or gym pictures, revealing hints of cellulite or sagging breasts, making sarcastic comments about someone displaying a 'healthy' appetite, 'flaunting their curves' or looking 'heartbroken'.

Even if they do not look at these kinds of magazines or the internet, little girls pick up on the anxiety around them. According to teachers and social science research, children as young as three years of age worry about their looks after watching their parents trying to make themselves look perfect in 'selfies'. They see their mothers taking ten photos to get the best angle, they hear the casual comments such as, 'Oh no, I look fat in that one, that's a terrible one', they see them using filters to alter their skin tone, to beautify out the wrinkles or lines. Little chil-dren are like sponges, picking up on everything around them, and girls in particular absorb this all-pervasive body anxiety. They learn early on that a woman's self-presentation – her weight, complexion, clothes – is one of the most important things about her.

Watch any of the millions of make-up tutorials on YouTube and you will realize just how identikit and synthetic 'perfect' beauty has become. For many girls and young women the daily routine starts with air-brushing out their natural skin tone, darker circles under the eyes, patches or blemishes, to create a very tanned blank canvas, and then layering on concealer, foundation, powder, contouring creams and highlighter.

Experimenting with cosmetics is, of course, a fun and harmless part of growing up. But it is sad to see individuals blanking out their natural radiance in favour of something so fake-looking, erasing the expressive, unusual quirks of their face, painting on dark eyebrows whatever their colouring, airbrushing out freckles and moles and hiding behind this barrier of war paint.

Digital images have created warped expectations of how normal skin should look. Compare your own bare face to any cosmetics adver-tisement and, for most of us, it is just not achievable. Even if you do not have spots, you probably have pigmentation or patches where your skin is lighter, darker or perhaps a little red. The more we cover up our natural faces, the further we drift away from what normality looks like. Of course, there's nothing wrong with wearing and enjoying make-up – I marvel at the transformation of my skin from my trusty BB (and CC!) cream, especially when I'm feeling tired or washed out. But when every day starts with a lengthy process of hiding and disguising our so-called 'flaws', it is inevitable that we will absorb the message there is something wrong with us. When it starts at such a young age too, we could be storing up a lifetime of body image anxiety ahead.

Self-objectification

It won't be news to you that we live in a culture where women are routinely judged on appearance, but do you know how deep and wide-ranging this bias is? Numerous studies carried out by economists and sociologists have proved that thinner women, who are perceived as more attractive, are promoted more quickly in all professions. Female attractiveness is a highly lucrative commodity – and unattractiveness is a significant disadvantage. US researchers call this the 'plainness penalty', finding that women with 'below-average looks' earn approximately 9 per cent less an hour than women rated as attractive.

Nor is this just the case in the fashion and beauty industries, where appearance is at least considered relevant. For women, being perceived as attractive is of overwhelming importance in every walk of life. And it's not just at work: research has shown that attractive children tend to be more popular and perform better at school, and attractive people are less often found guilty in court. Throughout our lives, looking good matters.

So what does 'looking good' mean – what does beauty look like to you?

Ditch the scales

Unsurprisingly, women who weigh themselves on the bathroom scales every morning report greater body dissatisfaction and have a more negative self-image than those who do not. As one reader told me, 'I weigh myself twice a day, every day. If the scales go up I've been known to go out for a late-night run just to shift a couple more pounds. I fight myself constantly. I am tired.'

This attitude and behaviour is, sadly, not unusual. But what's the addiction to scales all about? Why are we so obsessed with our weight and how can we ditch the habit?

Most women list eating less, exercising more and losing weight among their life goals, but the reality of losing weight is different and rarely makes us happy. As we have seen, many models with 'perfect' bodies are not content in themselves or even satisfied with their appearance. Depriving yourself of good nutrition is a wretched experience and genuine beauty does not depend on being thin. Every part of your body suffers when you are not consuming enough calories: undereating results in dry hair, dull skin, low mood and poor sleep. Hardly a recipe for physical health and wellbeing.

It's not easy, with our weight- and image-obsessed media, but weight must not become an overwhelming preoccupation. After suffering from anorexia for a decade, I no longer own a pair of bathroom scales. At long last I have learned to trust myself, to keep a balance, without recourse to that external judgement, those sinister numbers on the dial!

It is also essential to keep things in perspective. Normal body weight varies in every individual from day to day. Weight fluctuation is especially common in women at certain times of the month, when changes in levels of the hormones oestrogen and progesterone can cause fluid retention. You may have experienced breast tenderness, bloating or swelling before your period. This premenstrual water retention can result in a couple of kilos difference from one day to the next – and that's completely normal. It's not even weight gain or loss per se, but simply the kidneys reacting to falling levels of progesterone and passing out less fluid in the urine.

Think about this logically: you do not need to know your weight, to the nearest kilo, every day. As well as hormonal factors, there are plenty of reasons why your body may be slightly heavier or lighter – maybe you went out for dinner, maybe you just drank a litre of water – but it doesn't matter. You do not need to monitor this constantly. The outside world does not know, still less care, that you are a couple of kilos up or down on where you were yesterday, so why should you?

Look at your body in its entirety. Really look at it – your arms and legs, the skin, fat and muscles, skeleton, teeth and hair, not to mention around 60 per cent of our body that is made up of water. There is plenty of body to absorb those minor weight fluctuations: those few kilos go on all over! You are not livestock or bags of grain being sold at an auction. Your clothes, your mirror, your brain, your friends would tell you if you had gained or lost a serious amount of weight – other than that, let it be.

Of course, scales have a place in the doctor's surgery or if you are significantly underweight or overweight, but if this is not the case, consider getting rid of them. Nothing bad will happen, I promise you. It's liberating to be free of that self-imposed weigh-in on the bathroom scales. Ditching that daily dose of anxiety about the numbers will do your personal wellbeing and your body image a real favour.

Does body image matter?

Well yes, actually it does. Your mental attitude towards and private language about your own body matters immensely. A few years ago, a magazine survey reported that women have, on average, 13 negative thoughts about their appearance even before they leave the house every morning. That's a lot of negativity running in your head, a constant inner monologue of criticism, a cruel voice of self-loathing. And it takes its toll. If you start the day by telling yourself (or involuntarily hearing) that you are overweight, no amount of make-up will cover your dreadful skin, you look terrible in that outfit, is it any wonder your confidence is low? If you hate the way you look and constantly compare yourself to others, is it surprising that you end up feeling anxious or depressed?

Improve your body image

It is unrealistic to expect to feel physically confident and brimming with self-love all the time – we all have days where we feel unattractive or simply wrong. But if you feel consistently negative about your appearance, it's time to take action.

Start with a reality check. Are you physically active, can you walk and run, can you laugh and dance, talk to your friends, potter around the shops or hug your dog/cat/boyfriend/girlfriend? All these things are worth celebrating. Having a touch of cellulite, dodgy skin or a less-than-washboard-flat stomach should never be more important than these human experiences. Don't let those minor flaws take up your headspace.

If your body image is very poor, the problem isn't with your body; it's with how you think, feel and talk about it. Here are four good reasons to ignore the ugly voice.

- **It's unrealistic** to want the perfect body – presumably you have work, studies, family, your whole life, to be getting on with.
- **It's inaccurate** as what we think of as perfection is achievable by about 1 per cent of the population. This mythical perfection is usually part of an advertising campaign in which someone is trying to sell you something by making you feel inadequate. Anyway, most of the images of female and male beauty we see have been digitally retouched or altered in some way.
- **It's self-sabotaging** as, when we compare ourselves to others, we tend to compare up, not down, which further erodes our confidence. Why measure yourself against others? Animals don't compare themselves, they just get on with living their lives.
- **It's pointless** as being slim and beautiful doesn't protect you from pain, illness or heartbreak. Are gorgeous actors or models any happier than the rest of us?

Instead of fixating on your outer body, focus on developing your inner personality, your opinions, skills and interests. Don't forget that time and ageing get us all in the end and physical 'perfection' never lasts. What will you be doing in 10 or 20 or 50 years' time? When you're 80, will you remember the places you visited, the people you loved and the adventures you had in your life – or the times you managed to starve yourself down to a size zero?

Then there's body language. If we want to change the way we feel about our bodies, we could start by improving the way we talk about them. We will never be happy with ourselves when we are not happy in ourselves. The language of weight is loaded. Words we might use about ourselves are not always acceptable when used by others. Our view will differ – is 'skinny' offensive, is 'fat' insensitive, is 'curvy' a compliment or a euphemism? There are layers of implied judgement and approval behind most of the language we use.

As well as our negative inner monologue and our self-critical shared dialogue, we are surrounded by linguistic reminders that we are at war with our 'excess' flesh. If we aren't engaged in the 'battle of the bulge', we're being urged to 'conceal' and 'correct' flaws, to 'attack problem areas' and 'fight the flab'. The language of male bodies focuses on building strength, sculpting muscles and boosting endurance, whereas women are always trying to reduce, to slim down, to diminish. Is it any wonder that we dislike how we look when we are harangued from all sides with gym guilt, reminded of the virtues of trimming down, toning up, getting rid of our excess flesh?

Think of your friends who are different sizes. How would you describe their body shapes: sporty, slender, hourglass? Then think of the casual, abusive terms we use for our own bodies: jelly-belly, muffin top, bingo wings. Fairly light-hearted, you might think, but is it really funny? The way we talk about our bodies can have a corrosive effect on the way we feel about them. In our society, it is assumed that weight loss is a good thing. It's taken for granted that we all want to be thin and fat people hate being fat. How often do we hear 'You're lucky to be thin' or 'She's lost loads of weight and looks great' and so on.

Body image is complex, but your mental vocabulary is a good place to start. Try to eliminate negative or offensive terminology from your personal script. Don't use the words 'fat' or 'ugly' about yourself or others – ever. This applies to celebrities and strangers as much as yourself and your friends. Don't refer to your flabby bits, fat thighs, bingo wings or muffin top. Don't scrutinize or criticize other women; look for something beautiful in everyone. Try to find kinder language for your own body and focus on the quirks that make you unique. Can you appreciate your artistic hands, your captivating smile, maybe some freckles or a birthmark?

The droning self-critic is deeply ingrained in most of us and it takes time to break the habit. Kindness to oneself is a valuable life skill, one worth working on – and it makes you kinder to others. When you stop the verbal self-hatred, you'll stop the mental self-hatred.

What others say

Let's take a look at what others say about their body image.

❝ My body confidence isn't too bad, but I have quite a lot of self-doubt. I tend to boost my self-esteem with exercise. It's always been a way to feel good about myself and to clear my mind. I don't weigh myself regularly – that would definitely knock my confidence as I know I weigh quite a lot more than I used to when I was running. I prefer just to go by how I look and feel. ❞ **Emma, 29**

❝ In a nutshell: body image – hate; confidence – faked; self-esteem – none. Losing weight is a massive weight on my shoulders. I no longer look at myself in the mirror, I don't go shopping for clothes and I hate going out. Body image affects every aspect of my life. More than anything it would be the one thing I would change. I am my biggest critic and it leads to starving myself and weighing myself way more than I should. I do not think there is a minute that goes by where I don't think about it. ❞ **Gemma, 21**

❝ I think we all have our insecurities, don't we? I'm in a good place, but still want to work on it, step by step. When I look in a mirror, I try to spot things I like about myself rather than what I'm not happy with, because I know I can be my own worst critic. It's one of the things I'm working on: to go easy on me. I try not to scrutinize others but I'm only human and sometimes I find myself comparing myself with thinner girls, wanting to have a body more like theirs. Comparing is another thing that I still need to work on. I weigh myself regularly, every two weeks. It's just to get a general idea of where my weight is going. ❞ **Judith, 27**

❝ I do scrutinize other women's bodies but, usually, it's out of interest rather than to be critical or envious. I only know my body and I don't have many curves so it's interesting to see what other women look like and what clothes they wear to suit their shape. 〉 **Ali, 31**

〈 Everyone has things they want to change about themselves – don't they? I am slowly but surely working on building my self-esteem and embracing all my faults and insecurities. If I go on social media, however, and see a size 8 model on Instagram, I start to judge myself. 〉 **Taylor, 19**

〈 My body image is bad. I don't see the full picture, just the separate parts that make up my body, so I suppose I have quite a distorted body image. My self-esteem and confidence get boosted if I succeed academically or someone shows that they like who I am as a person. I am very critical of my body but am trying to accept it. I'm definitely very aware of other women's bodies and I make immediate comparisons. I weigh myself about three times a week when I'm at home, although I currently don't own bathroom scales. 〉 **Niamh, 18**

〈 My self-esteem and confidence are low. I am constantly critical of my own body and often find myself looking at other women's. My least favourite part is normally my thighs – they are huge – but at the moment, because I have gained so much weight, it is more or less everything. As regards my weight, I have specific numbers in my head that are just about 'acceptable' as an upper limit and I've passed them, so am in a crisis with that. Anything negative happening to me kicks off overexercise and undereating . . . Incessant running and a very controlled diet made me happy with my body. I was slim, had little to no fat and felt toned and confident. My legs were pure muscle and I often got compliments. I have a happy weight number, but it is near impossible to maintain. 〉 **Karen, 30**

〈 I would rate my confidence and self-esteem as quite low. I do have body image problems and I was always highly critical of myself, even as a toddler. I think I learned to take any and all of my anger out on my body, eventually growing to hate it. I avoid weighing myself because it's a constant reminder of my poor health, bordering on being underweight and that just escalates my anxiety. 〉 **Rue, 19**

❝ My relationships with the scales is unhealthy, but it's symptomatic of a much more complicated relationship with myself and my perpetual awareness of my own 'not-enoughness'. I've spent so much time and energy self-destructing. I've dedicated years and years of my life to my own shrinking, to trying to take up less space, to trying to be less, to be nothing . . . And yet I don't even think twice about the way other women look – I'm far more interested in the things they do, have done and hope to do. The things they say. The way they laugh. The choices they make. ❞ **Yasmin, 24**

❝ I don't like my body at the moment and recently I've been avoiding mirrors. I don't weigh myself as I'm not really sure what I want to achieve with that. I have put on weight in the last year and, while I'm not particularly happy about it, I'm not so unhappy that I feel the need to take major steps. I sometimes look at other women's bodies to try and work out how they're different from mine. Looking at others makes you appreciate just how weird and wonky we all are – even people I characterize as slim have odd curves or angles. ❞ **Letty, 29**

Some of these women's testimonies make me sad. I understand where they are coming from, of course. I've probably felt most of these negative emotions myself. Like many women, I have disliked my body and neglected my physical needs. But why is there such a chasm between the acceptance and appreciation we feel for other people's bodies and the self-critical, sometimes even self-loathing, language and sentiments we use to express our thoughts about our own? I once heard a very simple piece of advice on body image: be more critical of what you see in the media and less critical of yourself.

Remember those examples of your body from earlier in this chapter: as a house, the place in which you live; as a car, a machine that needs fuel to function; as a friend, whom you would never verbally abuse or deprive of food. You only have this one body and it's yours for life – fatter or thinner, richer or poorer, in sickness and in health. Treat it with respect. Don't go to war with yourself. Focus on self-acceptance and try to appreciate your body for what it does. That positive mental attitude shines out.

Finally, a word on beauty and body image. There is nothing beautiful about bitterness, envy, self-punishment or deprivation. We all know that the most attractive people are those who value themselves and care about others. They are more involved in the world around them so less concerned about how they look or what they weigh. They don't tell you how rough they're looking or how many kilos they've gained; they probably don't spend much time in a state of angst in front of the mirror. They may not be a perfect size 8. They may have cellulite or imperfect eyebrows. They may enjoy their food too much to bother with diets and never set foot inside a gym. They probably don't conform to society's aesthetic standards, but they're lovely, body and soul, because they are kind to themselves and others.

Think about self-care, nourishment and rest. Body image is not just about the exterior, the clothes and cosmetics you put on for the world or your dress size or your yoga selfies. Body image includes our hearts and brains and stomachs too. Take an holistic attitude: body image becomes a lot simpler when you remember that our bodies are what's going on inside as well as outside. Beauty is expressive and individual, not bland or conformist. After all, we wouldn't marvel at Everest or Niagara Falls if they looked identical to every other World Heritage Site. Stand naked in front of the mirror and marvel at your magnificent body, just as it is: perfectly imperfect and uniquely you.

2

Mood, confidence and self-esteem

'How are you?'

It's the simplest of questions, something we ask each other on a daily basis, yet, for most of us, the answer is far from simple.

'How you are' can depend on an almost infinite number of variables. Sleep, nutrition, hormonal fluctuations, the weather and the season, our physical environment, the people nearby, the journey to work, the smells, sights and sounds around us – all are factors that determine our psychological wellbeing on a daily basis. Physical sensations, financial worries or world news, close friendships and relationships, events in our family or workplace – these minor and major phases can shift around us hour by hour, constantly reshaping our mood and emotions. Something as simple as a lost phone, a slight disagreement with your mother, a stubbed toe, some days these little knocks can feel like the end of the world.

Frustratingly, we often do not know why we feel the way we feel. Seemingly insignificant events can affect our emotional balance without us even realizing it. Have you ever experienced that low feeling without really knowing why? When you go back over your day, you might realize that it was a criticism someone made at work, a comment on an Instagram post you shared, being ignored by someone you messaged on Tinder, even a glance from a stranger you interpreted as negative. Being ridiculously oversensitive is part of what makes us human. Misinterpreting other people's harmless comments is human. Having a bad night's sleep and feeling too tired to cope, that's human too.

'How you are' can be frustratingly inconsistent: one day you may have this emotionally functioning business nailed, feel positive, capable and fully on top of things, only to find yourself the next day anxious or overwhelmed. We are erratic creatures with irrational moods in an uncertain world – and there's no knowing what tomorrow will bring.

'How you are' is utterly individual: there are no rules for how circumstances will affect us personally. What causes you a sleepless night might not bother someone else, but that person might become stressed over something that you couldn't care less about. We tend to notice the resilience of others – 'Why can't I be as strong as they are?' – and underestimate our own.

'How you are' is also largely invisible. Most of us do not wear our hearts on our sleeves. From pride or fear or shame, we keep so much hidden and you cannot always know what another person is going through. Physical and emotional suffering doesn't always show. What if the person next to you on the bus or train has just been diagnosed with cancer? What if the colleague who sits opposite you is in the throes of a difficult divorce? What if the presenter who smiles from your break-fast TV screen has just suffered a miscarriage? I find this dimension of human beings both inspiring and moving: our hearts can be bursting with sadness or despair, yet we carry on.

From major life challenges such as illness or injury, to minor niggles like traffic delays or Twitter trolls, our everyday existence is fraught with potential highs and lows. Some days our emotional well-being can feel very fragile. Some days it's brave just to step outside your own front door!

Stress less

Stress is an unavoidable aspect of twenty-first-century existence and everyday life is filled with lurking stressors. In the modern era, stress is worn as a badge of honour. Like being 'too busy' to sleep or eat, being highly stressed is equated with being powerful and important. Resting is a sign of weakness and asking for time off is out of the question. We suffer in secret through stress-induced backache or migraine, we get skin rashes or panic attacks, we keep going until things get better or, worse, until we collapse.

The more we understand about stress on a physiological level, however, the more obvious it becomes that this is wrong. Insufficient sleep, excess caffeine, irregular eating, and, above all, prolonged strain are known to be highly damaging to the human body. We can cope with short bursts of stress or danger, but we are not designed to cope with it long term. Being wired all the time takes its toll.

Here's how the body responds to stress.

- The adrenal glands, just above the kidneys, begin to produce hormones.
- First, they pump out adrenaline and noradrenaline, to keep the body alert and focused.
- Then they pump out cortisol, which releases glucose from the carbohydrate glycogen stored in the liver and, when cortisol levels are high, breaks protein down to release energy, so we have the fuel needed to respond quickly.
- This adrenal response triggers the so-called fight-or-flight response. Heart and respiratory rate and blood pressure and alertness increase, our muscles tense, our senses become heightened and we get ready to escape or fight back.

When chronic stress repeatedly forces the adrenal glands to sustain high levels of cortisol, the adrenal glands become overburdened. They struggle to regulate hormones and excess levels of cortisol may damage healthy tissue. High levels of circulating cortisol play havoc with your appetite and encourage the body to store excess abdominal fat.

When stress gets too much, you may feel constantly exhausted and become reliant on stimulants such as caffeine, sugar or alcohol to keep you going. Adrenal fatigue may set in, causing weight gain, cravings, mood swings, insomnia, confusion, anxiety and depression. Extreme stress can cause stroke, heart disease and even death.

While we cannot entirely eliminate all sources of stress, we *can* reduce the impact they have on our physical and emotional wellbeing. The important thing is to recognize the warning signs when stress is becoming unmanageable and have strategies in place to help you cope. It could be as simple as relaxing in a hot bath or taking a nap. It could be taking gentle exercise, meeting up with friends or working from home. You may need a few days to yourself, away from other people and your smartphone. Your coping strategies will depend entirely on your own temperament. Making time in your life to unwind and de-stress should be a priority, not a luxury or a source of guilt. Stress should not be seen a badge of honour but as a warning sign that you need to take some time out.

Before the stress becomes overwhelming, slow down. Focus on what really matters: such as your own health, your family and the people you love. Taking stress seriously means giving your body the care it needs.

Hormonal havoc

Those ever-shifting emotional sands can be further upset at specific times. For women, these mood swings can be exacerbated by natural fluctuations of the monthly menstrual cycle, in a process known as premenstrual syndrome (PMS). In the week or ten days after ovulation and (if you are not pregnant) leading up to menstruation, levels of the hormones oestrogen and progesterone begin falling dramatically. These hormones, in turn, can interfere with brain chemicals, especially the mood-regulating hormone serotonin.

PMS has a physical as well as a psychological impact, with many women experiencing breast tenderness, water retention and abdominal bloating, fatigue, acne, sleeplessness, cramps, food cravings, constipation or diarrhoea, headaches and many other symptoms. Our emotional responses can become heightened, with extreme low mood, anger, irritation or weepiness.

PMS-related discomfort and emotional disruption is extremely common, with physical discomfort and emotional disruption affecting up to 85 per cent of women to some degree. It's a lot to contend with on a monthly basis and can have a real impact on our behaviour, bodies and mood. Even the calmest among us may have experienced emotional outbursts or irrational behaviour during that tense period prelude.

Escape routes ...

The American poet Sylvia Plath, well known for her emotional honesty, captured this sense of inner turmoil in her journal, asking, 'Is there no way out of the mind?'

Our minds are uniquely our own, yet they are not under our control. How can this be? Is there no way out? Whether it's unwelcome ruminations or incessant anxiety, it can feel impossible to control our own minds. Our worries mount up, our thoughts race and we end up panicky, sleepless or depressed.

Learning to control our minds is difficult but not impossible. The American writer Elizabeth Gilbert, in her book *Eat, Pray, Love*, considers it to be an essential skill: 'If you want to control things in your life so bad, work on the mind. That's the only thing you should be trying to control.'

Learning to regulate, or at least tune into, your mood and emotions, is worthwhile. Some emotional fluctuations – as we've seen in PMS – are unavoidable aspects of being human. We can experience highs and lows at any time of the month, however. It's important to get to know yourself and to understand your own emotional vulnerabilities.

What makes you feel good about yourself and what makes you feel bad? For example, being with certain friends might trigger negative feelings, making you feel insecure or worthless. Seeing a family member or ex-partner might cause you distress every time, arousing upsetting experiences from the past. Identifying the emotional impact of these toxic relationships is the first step to improving your emotional wellbeing.

It could be as simple as unfollowing some accounts on social media. I used to follow a lot of clean eating and 'fitspo' bloggers who were constantly tweeting their daily training regime, their workout selfies and their post-gym green juices. It's irrational, but seeing their posts made me feel inadequate because I hadn't started the day with a hardcore training session like them and I hadn't had a spirulina shot or a wheatgrass smoothie. They were skipping breakfast and pumping iron while I was enjoying coffee and maybe a croissant too . . . Removing them from my timeline was a relief – now I don't need to compare myself or start the day feeling like I've already fallen short. (See also Chapter 4, Social media and wellbeing.) Unfollowing unhelpful influences can be done quietly and tactfully. The individuals won't necessarily notice you've unfollowed them and it could save you a lot of unnecessary anxiety.

Self-limiting beliefs

As well as those unhelpful external influences, we often harbour internal beliefs that hold us back. These may be neuroses, past experiences or even childhood memories that we have somehow clung on to and they can be profoundly self-limiting. They stop us from pursuing new opportunities, putting ourselves forward for a promotion, asking someone out for a drink or just being brave and taking risks. These hang-ups also affect our self-esteem and emotional wellbeing at a deep level.

Self-limiting beliefs are often based on things that we were told in our formative years – comments made by parents or teachers about what we were and were not good at. Perhaps they referred to us as the 'academic one' or the 'sporty one' and these early labels tend to stick with us. Have you ever said or thought any of the following?

- 'I can't draw to save my life.'
- 'My brother is the brainy one in our family.'
- 'I never did get the hang of maths.'
- 'I'm just not a languages person.'
- 'I'm terrible at public speaking.'
- 'I've always been on the chubby side, even as a child.'

Here's a revolutionary thought: what if you've changed since you were bottom of your maths class? Could your running have improved since the day you came last in the egg and spoon race at school? What if you're now quite good at languages, but you just haven't tried? I'm quite different from how I was at seven years old and I bet you are too.

It is also important to separate events or skills from who you are as an individual. Too often we confuse what we do with who we are; we measure our self-worth by what we achieve in the outside world. In reality, exams or promotions are only external events, but we internalize these beliefs and allow them to define us in adult life.

Don't allow those memories of past weaknesses to develop into unquestionable truths. You are always changing and growing, and you can always improve. Nowadays, people go back to university in middle age, people retrain mid-career, so don't allow those early choices at school or university define who you are in adult life and the path you take.

To challenge those self-limiting beliefs, take a fresh perspective and ask yourself the following questions.

- Is this label or description or belief I hold about myself TRUE?
- How do I know it's true?
- When did I first start to believe it?
- Who told me this about myself?
- What evidence can I find to the contrary?
- How does this belief limit my life?
- What could I choose to believe instead about myself, which would move me forward?

Strategies for developing resilience

None of us can control events, but we can control how we respond to them. Developing emotional resilience is perhaps the most valuable thing you can do for yourself and is a skill that will serve you for the rest of your life.

Like any muscle, mental resilience needs regular attention and the more you work on it, the stronger it will become. As we have seen, when you are tuned in to your own emotional vulnerabilities, you can protect yourself better and strengthen that mental resilience muscle. You can avoid the toxic influences that bring you down. This works for physical vulnerabilities too: if you get to know your own warning signs, you can strengthen your resistance.

For example, working too hard might send you into a downward spiral and cause you to become anxious and depressed. Drinking too much alcohol might lead you to other dangerous habits, such as drugs or risky sexual behaviour. For me, starting a diet or buying some bathroom scales would be unwise because of my past struggles with anorexia. I know I'm fine as long as I don't start obsessing over numbers or calories. We're all different – and we are all strong and weak in different ways. Dieting or counting calories could be totally fine for you, but I would quickly get sucked back in.

Call it addiction, vulnerability or our Achilles heel, we all face different threats to our wellbeing. Moods and emotions are not easy to control, but they should not be completely uncontrollable. Every one of us has a choice over how we live our lives, who we spend time with, what we eat, how much we work, exercise and sleep. Above all, we can choose to take our mental health and wellbeing seriously.

Choose happiness

Is happiness really a choice? If so, why isn't it easier to feel happy? Why do we sometimes feel so damn sad?

We all encounter tough times in life – days, weeks or months when we feel directionless or demoralized. It can seem like everyone else is happier and more successful than us and we are all alone. But when these times come, as they will for us all, you are not as powerless as you feel. Even when you cannot change the situation, you can change the way you think about and react to it. Every one of us can make the choice to be positive.

There may be 'no way out of the mind', but we do not need to feel imprisoned in our own heads. It's remarkable what a difference our minds can make. One of the most powerful decisions you can make, whatever happens, is simply to remain positive. To find a bright side. To count your blessings no matter how numerous the challenges. On some days, positivity may come naturally; on other days, it will feel like dragging yourself through quicksand – but it is a choice. At the heart of this positive mindset is one small word: gratitude. Gratitude is a simple word and a simple act. Here are some of the reasons why gratitude makes sense.

- Gratitude is logical. Look at the world you inhabit, the warm clothes you are wearing, the food and drink around you, the roof over your head, all the possessions you own. Every one of us has a life of abundance compared with the majority of the world's population and we should be grateful for that.
- Gratitude is a magnet: like attracts like. Adopting a positive, welcoming attitude to what you have will attract more positivity into your life.
- Gratitude makes you see that what you have right now is enough. You never really need more than what you have in the present moment. Inhabit this moment and savour it.
- Gratitude is liberating. Being thankful is stronger than anger, regret or negativity. Even when things are over, even if they have ended badly, gratitude frees you for the future. When you can say 'thank you for the experience' you are able to forgive and move on.

- Gratitude helps you gain perspective. Remember that nothing stays the same for ever. Life will inevitably surprise you again in some unimaginable way. Don't assume that you're stuck with the way things are right now. You aren't: life can and will change in an instant.

Here are a few simple ways to incorporate gratitude into your life.

- **Make your gratitude all-inclusive, big or small** Appreciate everything and everyone in your life. Give thanks for the lessons you've learned, the people you've met, the love you've felt.

- **Track your gratitude** Make time at the end of every day to write down a few things you are grateful for. Don't worry if they seem relatively minor – some days it could be as simple as a shaft of sunlight on your face or a smile from a stranger. Don't overthink it. The point is simply to register the tiny moments of joy in daily life.

- **Give back** When a person or organization has helped you in some way, try to return, or at least acknowledge, their impact on your life. Writing thank you cards may be old-fashioned, but so what? And a box of chocolates or a bunch of flowers never disappoints!

- **Don't look back in anger** Ban what-ifs and if-onlys from your vocabulary. Just because something doesn't last for ever doesn't mean it wasn't good. Replace regret with a sense of wonder.

- **Let go of control** Remember that you cannot control what happens, you can only live for each moment. When you appreciate the present, you will feel less regret about the past and less anxious about the future.

- **Keep it simple** If you're struggling to feel gratitude, start with the simplest things: the grass between your toes, the wind in your hair, the rain on your face. Look around you and be mindful. There is always something to be grateful for.

Being mindful is a great skill and will give your wellbeing an instant boost. Being mindful simply means being aware of the world around you. It means tuning in to sights and sounds, the natural world, people and conversations, registering those moments of human interaction happening around you every day. It means savouring the first coffee of the day or the taste of toast and marmalade. It means staying open and curious and hungry. The more you notice the warp and weft of everyday life, the beautiful, unusual or downright quirky, the better your well-being will be and the more alive you will feel.

Don't succumb to despair. Don't lose yourself in social media. Don't let others get you down. You're in charge of your time, your body, your money, your energy, your outlook. As well as choosing happiness, think of all the other decisions that you – and only you – get to make!

Don't compare

If there's one thing guaranteed to lower your mood, it's comparing yourself to others. Comparison is meaningless and often self-destructive: first, because we usually compare up rather than down and, second, because we're often comparing ourselves with strangers. Have you ever found yourself wishing you could be more courageous, outspoken and self-assured? Comparing yourself to someone who seems bold and brave? Wanting to be more independent, less sensitive?

Stop right there. Remember that we never know other people's realities or what they are really going through. The self-confidence you envy in others could be quite fragile, it could be a defence mechanism, it could be a very brave face. The point is that we are all different, especially when it comes to our deepest, most private feelings. Different people are affected by different things. Our moods and emotional responses don't play by the rules. What bothers you may not bother others and, similarly, you may not give a moment's thought to something they worry endlessly about.

A friend of mine, also a writer, recently published a new book and received some scathing reviews online. She laughed when she told me about the negative feedback, attributing it to 'idiotic trolls'. I was amazed – and impressed. My confidence would have been clobbered. I'd have singled out the nasty comments, even among a million nice comments – and told myself I was a failure. My friend, however, has the confidence to see the negativity for what it is: 'Envy, probably, or they don't have anything better to do. I can't even be bothered to give them headspace.'

My friend takes a robust and admirable attitude to her work – but she isn't bulletproof either. I know that she suffers from terrible insecurity over her appearance, spends an inordinate amount of time on diets, losing and then regaining weight, and hates looking in the mirror. For all her professional confidence, her body image is very low. I don't diet, don't weigh myself and don't mind mirrors – whereas those same online comments could easily knock me off course. As always, comparison is meaningless, because we're different people. Her wellbeing is composed of different elements from my wellbeing: we're weak and strong in different ways.

The slings and arrows . . .

'How you are', that complex inner soup of moods and emotions, is constantly swirling and ever-changing. To be human is to face the 'slings and arrows' of life every day. Look around you, on the bus, in your school, university or workplace, in your favourite coffee shop. Other people look strong on the outside, right? And yet we are all surprisingly vulnerable. No amount of money, beauty or power can protect us from the challenges and setbacks of life. The miracle is not what we achieve during the good times, but that we don't go under during the bad times. Remember, no one else has it all sorted. That stunning friend of yours, that capable boss, that successful YouTuber you follow, they all experience the vicissitudes of life too, every day. Feeling overwhelmed or anxious, feeling like you've failed or let someone down or said the wrong thing . . . this is part of the human experience.

If it matters, it matters

Finally, if it matters to you, it matters. When you're feeling something, feel it. Try not to run away from your emotions, even when they are painful. Be robust and curious with yourself, challenge your self-limiting beliefs, examine the evidence and interrogate your responses. Look honestly at your lifestyle, your habits, your strengths and weaknesses. Invest time in developing your potential. Cultivate that inner resilience, learn what battles to fight and how to let things go.

But allow yourself to be human. Wellbeing is about tuning in to your emotions, not suppressing them. Accept the sad days and savour the happy ones. Open yourself to new experiences, places and people. Learn from successes and failures; grow through the highs and lows.

3

Depression, anxiety and obsessive-compulsive disorders

Depression

> Its tendrils threatened to pulverise my mind and my courage and
> my stomach, and crack my bones and desiccate my body. It went
> on glutting itself on me when there seemed nothing left to feed it.

According to the writer Andrew Solomon, depression is emotional pain
beyond sadness. Sadness such as grief is like being attacked by rust, which
weakens the structure of your mind. Depression is what happens when
the structure collapses. Solomon describes his own depression as a living
force trying to take him down.

In the developed world, around 1 in 4 of us experience depression
at some point in our lives. The question increasingly being asked is why
does a quarter of the population get depressed? Why do so many of us
who are better fed, richer and safer than humans have ever been suddenly feel so hopeless?

Although anxiety and panic disorders have profound effects on
our mental wellbeing, depression is another major challenge experienced by many of us. This may be intermittent periods of depression in
response to specific life events or traumas – so-called reactive depression
(previously often called exogenous – 'from without' – depression). Or
it may be a more constant, and perhaps more biologically based, sense
of sadness, darkness or internal despair (once referred to endogenous –
'from within' – depression).

John Geddes, Professor of Epidemiological Psychiatry at the University of Oxford, has called depression 'the single largest contributor to global disability that we have – a massive challenge for humankind'. The total estimated number of people living with depression worldwide increased by 18.4 per cent between 2005 and 2015 according to the World Health Organization, and the condition is now thought to affect over 320 million people worldwide. So what can be done about it?

The drug dilemma

The use of antidepressants and anti-anxiety medication has soared in recent decades. Annual data from NHS Digital shows that prescriptions for antidepressants have reached an all-time high, with 64.7 million prescriptions dispensed in England in 2016 – 3.7 million more than the 61 million items dispensed during 2015. It also represents an increase of 108.5 per cent on the 31 million antidepressants that pharmacies dispensed in 2006.

Antidepressant medication is based on the theory that depression and other mental illness occurs when brain chemicals are unbalanced. The medication acts on these brain chemicals – the all-important neurotransmitters that regulate mood – altering the balance and thus relieving the symptoms of depression. Scientific advances have greatly improved the drug options available and the current class of selective serotonin reuptake inhibitors (SSRIs) are safer and cause fewer side effects than the first generation of antidepressants – tricyclic anti-depressants (TCAs) and monoamine oxidase inhibitors (MAOIs). TCAs and MAOIs were often highly effective but also caused drowsiness, dry mouth, weight gain and other unpleasant side effects. Newer drugs in the SSRI class are better tolerated by patients, are thought to cause less dependency and help to alleviate mild to moderate depression and anxiety disorders.

The rise in prescribing of antidepressants is startling and raises questions of whether general practitioners (GPs) dispense antidepressants too freely and perhaps inappropriately. Are they handing out anti-depressants 'like smarties', as is sometimes alleged, using them as a sticking-plaster for when talking therapies are not available and creating dependency among the patients? Or is it that we are all becoming more open about mental health problems and therefore more willing to ask for help? The greater public awareness of mental illness and higher expectations among individuals for their own mental wellbeing is clearly a good thing, but it may also have contributed to the increased usage of medication.

Antidepressants remain a highly controversial topic, with clinical opinions divided as to their efficacy. While many believe they are worthwhile, others argue that such medications are little more than placebos – dummy pills that deceive us into thinking they are helping but have no active therapeutic benefit. Others even suspect drug companies of fiddling trial results in order to maximize profits.

A study published in early 2018 has been hailed as 'ground-breaking' in addressing this controversial area. The wide-ranging international investigation, led by the National Institute for Health Research Oxford Biomedical Research Centre, included all the published and unpublished data available. The scientists looked at results from more than 500 trials involving either a drug compared with a placebo, or several different medicines compared with each other. Weighing up efficacy and tolerability, the authors concluded that antidepressants are an effective tool for depression and should be far more widely available.

The study also highlighted the hidden nature of mental health conditions and pointed out that untreated depression is a huge cost to society. It reported that antidepressants and psychological therapies such as cognitive behavioural therapy (CBT) have similar success rates, with around 60 per cent of people reporting, within two months, about a 50 per cent reduction in their symptoms, particularly an improvement in mood and sleep. The researchers also pointed out that the scientific understanding of depression is still very imprecise and new treatments are badly needed.

Should you take medication for anxiety, depression or other mental illnesses? It's a deeply personal choice. Just as some people take pain-killers for a headache and others don't, the decision about anti-depressants is one that only you can make. There are countless testimonies out there showing that medication has helped many thousands of anxious, depressed or even suicidal individuals, relieving the worst of their symptoms and even saving their lives. But only you can decide what's right for you. You may happily swallow your tablets and not think twice about it, you may take them but prefer not to tell anyone or you may decide they are not for you and instead pursue psychological therapies or alternative treatments.

Some people are reluctant to take medication because they are ashamed to admit that anything is wrong in their life, that they can't cope. Popping a pill makes them feel like they are 'giving in'. But this couldn't be further from the truth: remember, it's strong to seek support for mental illness, not weak. And it's important not to make moral judgements about treatment: just as you would seek medical help for a physical illness, so you should seek medical help for a mental illness too. You wouldn't 'tough it out' with cancer or a broken leg, and nor should you suffer through panic, depression or anxiety. No one should judge you for taking antidepressants, nor should you judge yourself. The treat-ment you need may be medication, talking therapies or a combination of the two.

Speaking personally, I can see both sides. I took fluoxetine hydro-chloride (also known as Prozac) for several years and it helped me through a very dark time. In my case the primary issue was anorexia, but Prozac is widely used for depression and obsessive-compulsive and panic disorders. When I began to recover mentally and physically from the eating disorder, however, I was keen to reduce my dosage and gradually to come off the drug altogether. It had provided much-needed stabil-ization of my brain chemicals when I was extremely underweight and emotionally fragile. I don't feel it was weak to take medication during a difficult period of my life, but I was glad to stop taking it eventually.

If you decide on medication for your depression or anxiety, you may need to try several different kinds before you find the right one. Finding the right drug and dosage is more a matter of trial and error than an exact science. Be patient and don't give up hope: most anti-depressants take several weeks to start working. You should also be careful and consistent with your medication, and not mix it with alcohol or recreational or other non-prescribed drugs. You should not discontinue the medication too soon after you start to feel better – it is generally advisable to continue taking it for a few months after the symptoms improve. It is estimated that about 80 per cent of people stop antidepressants within a month, which is far too soon.

You should also never discontinue medication suddenly or without medical advice as this can be dangerous and cause a relapse; instead you should taper the medication down gradually. Above all, you should take the medication exactly as prescribed, contact your GP or psychiatrist with any concerns or side effects and have regular reviews of how you are feeling.

Anxiety

Anxiety is a form of stress, but it is usually more serious than the stress most people experience in everyday life. Feeling stressed is a recurring theme in our daily language: we get stressed by traffic jams and packed trains, slow Wi-Fi speeds and bad customer service; we get stressed out by a disagreement with our boss or our mother; we find it stressful preparing for a job interview or a first date.

These types of stress are normal and inevitable. We all have niggling worries and concerns and we all experience stresses and strains. These might be caused by those minor hassles, such as traffic or commuting to work, or they might be more significant, such as illness, family problems or financial trouble. Unfortunately, these are unavoidable aspects of adult life.

Constant stress and severe anxiety are not normal or inevitable, however. They are damaging to your health and wellbeing, and should be taken seriously. They can affect many different areas of your life, including your mood and emotions, your cognitive functioning, relationships with friends and partners, everyday behaviour and activity levels, your career, studies or exam performance and your physical health.

With the common, everyday form of stress, most of us do cope most of the time – even if it sometimes feels as if we are only just keeping our heads above water. Maybe we moan about it to friends or on social media, but the stress doesn't stop us from sleeping at night and it doesn't impair our daily functioning. When the worrying becomes uncontrollable, however, or challenges feel insurmountable, this can develop into severe and disabling anxiety.

There is no clear dividing line between 'normal' and 'abnormal' levels of worry, but there are indicators that anxiety may be getting out of control. Here are some of the signs to look out for.

- Your anxiety is starting to affect your physical health. You may experience a repeated physical response to anxiety, such as back pain, insomnia or migraine.
- You may find yourself obsessing over minor events: an offhand comment from a colleague, for example, or a trivial disagreement with a friend. You know it's not important but you can't stop turning it over in your mind.
- Your anxiety is unproductive. You're thinking and worrying about a problem but you're not getting anywhere. Anxiety is unhelpful because it does not actually help you fix the situation.
- You are ruminating, usually over things that have already happened or things that might happen in the future. These may be minor events, but when you are in a state of anxiety the worrying can take up hours or days of your time.
- You feel stuck. Sometimes anxiety becomes so severe that you forget what kicked it off in the first place. You may experience circular thoughts and feel stuck in a loop of repetitive worry.
- Your anxiety involves regret or anger or a feeling of being wronged

or misunderstood. We know we cannot change the situation so we end up feeling powerless.

- It's habitual – you're anxious more often than not – and troubling. It may be interfering with your daily life, preventing you from seeing friends, going out or working. It may also be stopping you from sleeping.

You may not be able to pinpoint the starting point and it may not have a single cause: worrying about a lot of things is known as 'generalized anxiety'.

Remember that everyone is different. Some of us are naturally more anxious than others, some of us are overthinkers, some of us get nervous before big events, some dwell unnecessarily on the past and go over and over things. Even among your friends and family you can probably identify the natural worriers from the lucky laidback ones!

Simply feeling anxious does not make you abnormal. In the modern era, surrounded by busy roads and fast cars, suspicious strangers and other risks, we need to be on the alert at all times. Without a sensible level of anxiety we would not be watching out for those potential dangers – a mugger or a speeding lorry, say. Threats of terrorism, bombings or mass shootings are all over the news and our daily freedoms are constantly being affected in the name of 'national security'. Sadly, we are aware we could be caught up in tragedy at any time. And we need stress even for the non-dangerous occasions: the racing heartbeat and clammy palms are your body's adrenaline response to nerves, helping you 'gear up' to perform at your best for a speech, an interview or an exam.

But living with constant and severe anxiety is different. Over time it affects your physical as well as your mental health and can undermine your confidence in your ability to study, work or form relationships with others. It isn't OK if you are anxious most days or if you wake up feeling worried even before you have properly begun the day. If you feel powerless to change your situation or if you do not even know what you're worrying about but still feel intensely worried, that isn't OK either.

If your anxiety is altering your normal behaviour, it may cause you to isolate yourself, drink excessive amounts of alcohol or take drugs, become aggressive or withdrawn, experience prolonged low moods, harm yourself or feel suicidal, which are all important warning signs. When worry and anxiety reach this level, you can and should feel able to ask for help (see the additional sources of support at the end of the book).

What are we so anxious about?

Although anyone can suffer from anxiety and stress, it seems that some groups may be more vulnerable than others. Studies over the past few years have highlighted a worrying increase of mental illness among young women. In 2016 and 2017 this led to an explosion of alarming newspaper headlines. In 2016, the *Daily Telegraph* reported 'soaring numbers of young women suffering mental health problems and self-harm' and, in 2017, they asked, 'Why are so many of Britain's teen girls struggling with mental health problems?' In 2016, *The Times* newspaper reported 'Young women in Britain suffering record levels of depression, post-traumatic stress and self-harm' and *The Guardian* covered an 'Alarming spike in psychiatric disorders in young women'.

Those newspaper headlines followed a major NHS report in 2016, which found that more than one quarter of young women were suffering from symptoms of common mental health problems such as anxiety, panic and depression. Health officials said that they were particularly concerned about the trends in the youngest age group – that is, those aged 16–24 – who are growing up in the era of social media and all kinds of stresses.

In the Introduction to this book I mentioned the depressing findings from countless surveys and research projects over the past few years. In 2018 a survey by the Prince's Trust reported that British youngsters are the 'unhappiest generation in a decade', with 3 out of 5 young people aged 16–25 regularly feeling stressed over jobs and money. One in four said they felt 'hopeless' on a regular basis and nearly half had experienced a mental health problem. Also in 2018 psychologists at the University of Bath reported findings from a study of more than 40,000 students and found that perfectionism – excessively high personal standards and overly harsh self-criticism – was more prevalent among this generation than any previous one, causing chronic stress and a sense of hopelessness.

But perfectionism, chronic stress and hopelessness are not the worst of it. According to the Samaritans, 'the rise in people feeling suicidal, attempting to take their own life and self-harming is alarming.' This increase is particularly notable in young women. Although young men are still the group most likely to commit suicide, recent findings from the World Health Organization reveal that women are twice as likely as men to develop certain mental health conditions such as panic and anxiety disorders, depression and eating disorders. Women are also two to three times more likely to attempt suicide (although four times more men than women die from suicide).

And it's not only young women: in 2017 the National Society for the Prevention of Cruelty to Children (NSPCC) reported that the telephone helpline Childline was helping a record number of suicidal children and teenagers, with children as young as ten struggling with thoughts of ending their own lives. In 2014 Childline gave nearly 17,800 telephone counselling sessions to children talking about suicide. The number rose to nearly 19,500 in 2015, and to more than 22,400 in 2016 – an increase of 15 per cent, which was the highest level the charity has ever recorded.

Clearly, this so-called 'generation perfection' (and those coming up behind them) are facing a very modern set of anxieties and feeling the pressure. Most of those struggling with mental health problems cite academic and social pressures, concerns over jobs and money, and unrealistic expectations from the online world that make them feel they should be perfect.

Wearable anxiety

Can we ever escape it? This modern anxiety is exacerbated by the amount of scrutiny we are under and, arguably, more self-examination and analysis than ever before. When you consider the amount of personal data, performance and biofeedback we can measure, it's no wonder we judge ourselves so harshly.

Our phones, for example, are no longer simple communication devices, but instead instruments that monitor our daily lives. I recently got a new smartphone and, after a few days of playing around with it, trying to figure out various new functions, I realized that the little trainer icon on the home screen was actually a built-in pedometer. So far it has proved impossible to disable – whether I like it or not, the phone is walking around with me and counting my steps.

This is hardly a disaster, but it can make me anxious. The current health advice is that we should be walking at least 10,000 steps a day. If I have been writing all day, for example, I feel lazy at my disastrously low step count. Here's my thinking process: I may have written 2,000 words but I've barely walked 200 steps. This is awful. I'm such a sloth . . . and so on. (We should, of course, remember that our brain is a very hungry organ and consumes around 20 per cent of our resting daily calories!) Or maybe I've gone for a long bike ride (not counted) or a swim (not counted) or I've simply gone out without my phone!

Pedometers are old news, but our smartphones are at the forefront of physiological measuring and monitoring. They make the perfect spies: they are digitally advanced and with us virtually all the time. Activity trackers like FitBit are embedded with accelerometers and altimeters, calculating the number of stairs climbed, calories consumed and breaths taken. They will even collate your daily data to produce in-app graphs if that's your thing. The technology offers constant upgrades and new developments, including sensors to track sleep apnoea, earbuds to measure how much you sweat, wearable blood glucose meters and personal hydration monitors. Big Brother is watching you indeed.

This so-called 'wearable' technology feeds into a movement called 'the quantified self' – or life-logging – which believes in self-knowledge through self-surveillance. This involves tracking data from our own bodies at all times, from the gut microbiome to galvanic skin responses to cardiovascular activity to sleep patterns. 'Quantified Selfers' believe that this constant input of homeostatic data builds a complete picture of who you are, and can help to optimize performance, expand potential and eliminate risk.

Digital health is set to become an even larger part of our lives. In the USA the sales of digital wearable medical devices are expected to exceed $55 billion in 2022, an increase from $10.5 billion in 2017/2018. Worldwide, over 165,000 health-related apps are available that aim to help with everything from brushing our teeth more effectively and sleeping more efficiently to achieving superior orgasms. Alongside diet, fitness and mindfulness apps, the message seems to be that a better, healthier you is only a few data points away.

It's exhausting just to think about. Not only do we have all our social media channels to keep up with and our perfect online lives to curate, but we are also facing a tsunami of physiological performance reports daily, nightly, providing yet more sources of comparison and anxiety.

So is there anything wrong with data logging? Of course self-awareness is important, and information is power, but when it comes to health and wellbeing you can go overboard. You do not need to know the exact number of calories in every morsel that passes your lips or the exact number of steps you have taken every day. Recent studies have found that fitness or calorie-counting apps are commonly linked to 'eating disorder attitudes and behaviours', and many users experience intense anxiety when they underperform or do not meet their daily targets. Your wearables may be tracking your physical activity but they cannot measure your emotional wellbeing. A balanced active lifestyle is happier by far than an obsessive guilt-fuelled one.

Female or male, adolescent or adult, with or without our FitBit or Jawbone fitness trackers, it's clear that anxiety is an escalating problem in the twenty-first century. So why might this be? Here are a few of those voices on what's making them anxious:

> ❛ There's massive pressure on young women to look and act a certain way. There are very strict guidelines on what is considered "acceptable" and as soon as you feel you don't look this certain way, the anxiety comes along . . . This little voice in your head of not being good enough . . . then depression and hating what you see in the mirror. ❜
> **Gemma, 21**

> ❛ My generation of women have grown up feeling like life is a linear set of "right decisions" and success equates to being a certain way, even if this way isn't right for us. I think it can cause anxiety and depression, especially when we don't feel empowered to make decisions, take different paths or really understand what's right for us . . . there is a major fear of making a mistake. My worst periods of anxiety and depression have been when I've felt like I've had no control over my life. ❜ **Letty, 29**

> ❛ I'm far too familiar with anxiety and depression . . . Society has created this definition of "perfection" that everyone is trying to fulfil – but it doesn't exist! ❜ **Taylor, 19**

> ❛ Young women today are under increased pressure to "be everything" – to perform well academically, to be beautiful, to be "strong enough" to compete with the boys, to be sporty and active, to be arty and creative, to possess talents that span far and wide. And nowhere in all that teaching are we ever taught how to be resilient and realistic, and how to respect ourselves throughout that. ❜ **Yasmin, 24**

The recurring themes in these experiences of anxiety and depression are the many choices we have, how to make the 'right' decisions in our lives and worry about having, or not having, control. Then there's the pressure from society and the media to look and be a certain way (which is explored in greater detail in Chapter 4, Social media and wellbeing).

Many of the women whose experiences are included in this book also express complex emotions around food and eating, their body shape and weight. These issues play a significant role in the rise in eating disorders among young women, as we will see in Chapter 5, Nutrition, diet and wellbeing.

Fear, anxiety and bravery

Fear is a strange emotion because it is often completely imaginary, with no basis in reality. That is, truly fearful situations are rare – when did you last face a raging lion or a mass murderer? And yet our minds invent all sorts of things to fear and then torment us with how on earth we would cope. Nowadays the threats we face are usually not life and death situations or even physical peril, but existential anxieties can be just as distressing. We lie awake fearing all sorts of things – financial ruin, serious illness or sudden bereavement – increasing our own anxiety as we add dread upon dread.

Mercifully, these fears do not often materialize – and when they do happen, we do cope. We tend to underestimate our own capacity to deal with crises, but when they are actually happening, we have no choice but to get on with it. The fear comes from the anticipation and the what-ifs, but in the moment we are surprisingly strong, even brave. Every time we cope with what life throws at us, this takes strength and bravery.

It is important to remember that, whatever happens, you will survive. Human beings have an amazing capacity to just keep going. We may feel weak, unable to cope and beset by anxiety, but we don't give up. The challenges will be different for each of us, depending on our personal circumstances. I remember the stratospheric levels of anxiety I used to experience before a social meal with friends: I was gripped with fear about eating out in public for days beforehand. Bravery is bravery, whether it takes the form of climbing Mount Everest, giving a presenta-tion to a roomful of colleagues or just getting dressed and leaving the house. For me, just turning up to the restaurant and surviving the ordeal, I mean meal, took all my courage. You are courageous every time you do something that scares or challenges you or makes you want to run away.

Fear and nerves are normal, whether or not you have a specific mental health condition. There are several ways to cope.

- **Accept that fear is part of life** At some time, almost everyone feels it.
- **Reframe threats as challenges** Think of them as opportunities to grow. You're not scared, you're excited.
- **Try to avoid the perfectionist mindset** No one is ever perfect. If you never make mistakes, you will never learn. Embrace failure as a chance to improve.
- **Count down** When I get super-nervous about a forthcoming event, I tell myself, 'In 24 hours this will be over; whatever happens, I just have to get through the next 24 hours.'
- **Keep things in perspective** It's easy to let minor fears (for example, public speaking) rage out of control. It's nerve-wracking, yes, but it's not life and death.
- **Ask yourself, 'What really matters?'** Health and home, family and friends, food and water. If you have all those things, you're doing fine.
- **Be bullish, be brave** Challenge yourself on those fears: what's the absolute worst that could happen?
- **But don't catastrophize** The likelihood is that everything will not go wrong. Adopt a new mantra: 'Everything will be OK in the end. If it's not OK, it's not the end' (attributed to John Lennon).
- **Breathe** Deep breathing slows your heart rate, supplies oxygen to your anxious brain, calms you down and clears your mind.
- **Above all . . .** remember that, whatever happens, you'll be OK.

Fear is rooted in self-doubt. Underlying most of our fears is a fundamental lack of trust in ourselves. Don't allow fear and anxiety to take over: instead, look at the facts and look at how you have coped in the past. Really focus on the reasons underlying your fears and try to find the evidence. Take, for example, public speaking: you may feel sick and shaky beforehand, but it's unlikely that you will actually run screaming from the room. Or a first date: it might be nerve-wracking meeting this guy or girl, but the chances are that they're nervous too. You've never actually been tongue-tied on previous dates, have you? When you look at your past behaviour you will realize that you always cope (and often enjoy yourself). Try to believe in yourself. Practising, training and strengthening that self-belief muscle is essential for every aspect of your wellbeing. See Chapter 2, Mood, confidence and self-esteem for how to challenge those self-limiting beliefs.

This does not, however, mean denying your own vulnerabilities. We are all vulnerable: that's what makes us human. But we are also strong, adaptable and resilient. When we are fearful about future events, when we start to visualize calamity and failure, we are really doubting our own resilience and ability to cope. And this is why it bears repeating (some days I have to repeat it to myself multiple times!): whatever happens, you'll be OK.

Panic

Fear and nerves are normal, but if your anxiety feels overwhelming, it may tip over into panic or a panic attack. During a panic attack you may feel extremely scared, tense or unwell. You may feel overwhelmed with terror and experience physical symptoms such as sweating, hyper-ventilating or dizziness. You may try to escape the stressful situation or even feel paralysed. During a panic attack, individuals often feel that they might faint or collapse and in severe episodes you might believe you are about to have a stroke or heart attack.

Some panic attacks can be linked to a specific phobia, such as snakes or heights. In social phobia, panic is triggered by a harmless social situation, such as a party, or a build-up of emotional distress, overthinking and anxiety. The most common type of phobia is agora-phobia, in which individuals experience panic on buses, in shops or in large crowded places.

It is estimated that around 1 in 10 people have experienced a panic attack at some time in their life. Although you may feel very self-conscious and conspicuous during an episode of panic, it's not always obvious to outsiders. As we have seen, a common feature of both anxiety and panic attacks is downplaying one's own ability to cope – under-estimating what you can do to control your mental and physical fears. This in turn exacerbates the sense of panic. Another common feature is the lack of logic: rationally, you know the fear is not logical but you still feel it.

The panic or phobia is inevitably self-perpetuating so the more you avoid a situation, object or event, the more fear you feel towards it. This is especially true for social phobia, where isolating yourself only leads to further isolation and avoiding the company of others only increases the anxiety you feel about social interactions. However intense your anxiety, it is essential to maintain social links, even if these are just with a few close family members and friends.

Obsessions and compulsions

OCD has two main features: obsessional thoughts and compulsive behaviours.

Obsessional thoughts

Obsessional thoughts are when you find anxieties or distressing ideas or images circling round and round inside your head. The thoughts feel completely uncontrollable – indeed, the more you try not to think about them, the more they dominate your brain. Obsessive thoughts may centre on things that have happened in the past and can range from the most mundane event to serious traumas. The more you try to block out the thoughts or memories, the more aware you become of them and the less able you are to make them stop.

Obsessional thoughts may centre on a fear of harming oneself or others. These can feel vivid and quite realistic, such as visualizing yourself hurting a family member or attacking a stranger, even though you have never been violent or aggressive. Such thoughts are highly distressing.

In their milder form, obsessional thoughts are similar to the anxiety discussed earlier, where thoughts and worries circulate on a repetitive loop around your brain, escalating and making you feel unable to cope or 'change the record'.

It is important to understand that obsessive thoughts do not need to be violent or dramatic to be upsetting. If they are repetitive and feel uncontrollable, they are by definition obsessive. Even if they do not restrict your daily life, it is likely they will be affecting your mood and emotions.

Compulsions

Obsessive thoughts are sometimes (but not always) accompanied by compulsive behaviours. Repeating a series of ritual actions can feel like a way of controlling obsessional thoughts and somehow keeping things safe.

The most common forms of compulsions are checking, counting and cleaning. Individuals may repeatedly check the oven is switched off, the front door is locked or the lights are turned out. They will go back and check many times over, needing the reassurance that the locked door is actually locked or the oven is off. Cleaning takes various forms, from scrubbing the floors to repeatedly washing themselves. This is usually linked to a fear of contamination and a horror of everyday germs, especially in public places. Compulsions also take the form of mental rituals, such as repeating particular words or phrases or counting to a certain number.

Compulsive actions are often accompanied by a sense of responsibility and guilt. The individual fears that if they do not, for example, count to 100 between every bite of food something terrible will happen to a loved one. Counting or setting things in the 'correct' order is somehow going to make things right.

Like obsessive thoughts and fears, the individual is logically well aware that their compulsive behaviours are not rational. They know their rituals are not helping. They acknowledge that they do not make sense. They know the more checking or cleaning they do, the more locked into it they become. As with obsessive thoughts, however, individuals feel powerless to control their compulsive behaviour, at the same time as needing rigid control over everything around them. In a way, the compulsive behaviour is both a crutch to cope and a trap that the person cannot escape.

When it gets serious

Just like anxiety, obsessive-compulsive behaviours can be seen on a spectrum. We all feel some anxiety in our daily lives: we all know the nervous, nauseous feeling before giving a speech or presentation in public and we have all felt the intense shyness of walking into a party alone. The same goes for OCD: we all have habits, routines and strange quirks.

When anxiety, panic or obsessive-compulsive disorders take hold, however, they can seriously interfere with your everyday functioning. They begin to restrict your life, preventing you from socializing or going for new opportunities at work. They sap your confidence and affect everything you do. They gradually take over, narrowing your horizons, because you cannot cope with the unexpected or random nature of the outside world. Being plagued by repetitive thoughts or compelled to repeatedly carry out particular checking or cleaning routines is exhausting for both mind and body.

Remember that mental wellbeing matters as much as physical wellbeing. Obsessive thoughts and compulsive behaviours, whether trivial or traumatic, interfere with your peace of mind. But no matter how out of control your head feels, all is not lost.

Meditation

'If you want to conquer the anxiety of life, live in the moment, live in the breath', says the Indian author and spiritual teacher Amit Ray.

It is distressing to feel that one's mind is out of control. I know how frustrated I become when I'm not able to control my worries or racing thoughts, which only exacerbates the anxiety loop. We feel annoyed and impatient with ourselves: of all people, we should be in control of our own thoughts, shouldn't we? Who are these gremlins causing havoc inside your head? It's confusing and upsetting when your mind seems to have run away with itself.

Meditation has both physical and emotional benefits and, together, they will help slow your thoughts and calm you down. Even the simplest meditation techniques can make a real difference to getting on top of anxiety, panic, obsessions and compulsions. They can help you regain control and restore that elusive peace of mind.

Our breathing speeds up when we become anxious, which fuels those fight-or-flight and panicky sensations. Calming down starts with deep and regular breaths in and out, inhaling and exhaling, holding and releasing. Slow and rhythmic breathing delivers much-needed oxygen to the brain and relaxes every muscle in your body. While you are con-centrating on the rhythm of your breathing you will have less mental space for worry. Meditation gives your overactive brain a place to put all those anxious thoughts, especially when you are replaying past events or worrying about the future.

Meditation not only calms you in the moment, but also helps you deal with stress more effectively in other areas of your life. It triggers a positive relaxation cycle within the body, as we take oxygen in and release tension out. Small irritations or setbacks will feel more manage-able; anxiety or anger will be less automatic. Think of it as a virtuous circle spreading into your life, improving all aspects of your physical and mental operations!

You will find more detailed guidance online, with thousands of apps, as well as books and CDs available. There are different types of meditative practice, from simple to more structured, so try out a few techniques and see what suits you. I use meditation at night for insomnia, and my meditation varies depending on my mood. Sometimes I just lie in bed and focus on my breathing, sometimes I'll use a guided meditation app and sometimes I'll actually light a candle and sit in the lotus position. You may like to meditate at night to prepare you for sleep or first thing in the morning to clear your mind for the day ahead. Whatever works for you is fine: remember that there is no right or wrong way to get peace of mind.

If meditation doesn't work for you at first, persevere. We tend to believe that meditation should be effortless but it rarely is – I'm always surprised at how hard I need to concentrate in order to meditate effect-ively! This isn't about just letting your thoughts float away to some fluffy place in the clouds. It demands time and attention and the more you practise, the more powerful it becomes.

Meditation can be integrated seamlessly into the simplest of tasks as you go about your day. If sitting cross-legged in silence or lying down with your eyes closed doesn't work for you, try a more natural approach. Walking meditation, gardening, baking or even cleaning meditation can also promote equilibrium and give you headspace in your daily life. The technique is simple: whatever you are doing, simply focus on the task at hand. If you're gardening, feel the weeds as you pull them out of the ground and the sensation of grass under your feet (barefoot if possible). If cooking, focus on the process of sifting the flour and folding in the eggs. Watch the streaks and shine as you clean the windows or the pat-terns on the carpet as you vacuum. Breathe deeply and try to clear your mind; focus on the task at hand and nothing else. Getting absorbed in a physical chore, no matter how mundane, can be deeply restorative. It's like a time-out from anxiety and monkey-brain!

Even when that meditative state does not come easily, it is worth persevering. Research shows that it can alleviate depression, anxiety and a range of other mental health challenges. Whether you use it to help with any of these conditions, calm you when panic takes hold or simply to relax and recharge, meditation is a potent tool. It's healthy, it's free – and best of all, it's entirely private! It's all going on inside your head, so you can use it anytime and anywhere.

Insomnia and anxiety

Just like the old saying that misery loves company, there is no doubt that anxiety loves insomnia. Anyone experiencing anxiety tends to find it even worse at night: when there are none of the external distractions of the day, that mental churn can circulate, escalate and seriously interfere with your sleep. And nights are dark and often lonely – somehow everything seems worse when it's 3 a.m. and you're exhausted and desperate to switch off. Even though many other people in your street, neighbourhood or town are actually experiencing insomnia too – and this is a fact – it feels like the loneliest experience in the world.

Whether you struggle with falling asleep (sleep onset) or staying asleep (sleep maintenance) it's clear that anxiety is not a good bedfellow. The meditation and relaxation strategies outlined above are ideal for your evening wind-down and perfect for practising in the peace and quiet of your bedroom as you prepare to drift off. It's also worth referring to Chapter 8, Sleep, for more detailed advice on sleep hygiene, bedtime routines and disconnecting at night.

A way out?

Mental illness can feel all-consuming at times, like a waking nightmare or a maze with no way out. It's important to keep it in perspective, however. Like many other illnesses, it is temporary and it can be treated. You were not born with depression or anxiety and they are not part of your core personality. Obsessive habits or compulsions, no matter how troubling they have become, do not define you. You can and will get back to a life free from this overwhelming sadness or stress.

As well as seeking the right treatment, whether that is medication, talking therapies or a combination of the two, there are immediate ways to improve your wellbeing. Prioritizing your own health is important, as is acknowledging when you are struggling. Don't minimize what you're going through. Remember, if it matters, it matters.

Then commit to taking action. Tackling anxious feelings is a good place to start, since anxiety is often the driver for low mood, panic and obsessive behaviours. No matter how bad you are feeling, practising a few daily routines can be surprisingly effective. With or without other psychological intervention, try these simple tactics.

- **Reduce your body tension** Deep breathing, relaxation and meditation are highly effective techniques for calming yourself down and reducing your anxiety levels. Slowing your breathing and relaxing your muscles naturally reduces the physical tension you are holding in your body. Anxiety control training (ACT) and progressive muscle relaxation (PMR) are based on the premise that muscle tension is the body's psychological response to anxiety-provoking thoughts.
- **PMR** This is a routine that you can easily do at home, for example while lying on the sofa or in bed before sleep. It involves tensing specific muscle groups throughout your body, from your feet and calves all the way up to your shoulders, neck and face muscles. You clench the muscles tightly, feeling the tension and then releasing it, noticing how it feels when you relax the muscles. Relaxing the muscles helps to block the anxiety-provoking thoughts, as well as promoting a sense of intense relaxation and wellbeing.
- **Change your focus** Make the decision that you won't dwell on upsetting memories or thoughts. Tell yourself firmly that you are not going down that path. Remind yourself that these are minor events, and in a few weeks' time they won't matter at all.

- **Detach** If the distressing or recurring thought really won't go away, just watch it. Don't get involved, just observe with interest. Keep yourself emotionally detached and watch with interest how the thoughts and images come and go through your brain. Again, yoga and relaxation techniques can really help with this process of detachment.

- **Concentrate** When you find yourself becoming anxious, concentrate hard on something else. Whether it's tedious housework, revision or watching TV, try to focus hard on what you are actually doing in the present moment. As we've seen, even mundane cleaning or cooking can be meditative. Don't allow the anxious thoughts to dominate.

- **Distract yourself** Find something completely different to take your mind off the worry and away from the panic. It could be a fun, exhausting or difficult activity – you can't worry about the past while you're learning to dance! Other simple distraction techniques include ringing a friend or just going for a walk – changing your physical state really will help to change your mental state.

- **Challenge yourself** Stand up to those repetitive thoughts, and answer back! Try to take a fresh perspective on the same old self-destructive dialogue when it starts. Question your assumptions: did that person really mean to hurt you with that comment? Does flunking your driving test really mean you're a complete failure? Will the interview really be as bad as all that – and so what if it is? See if you can counter the habitual negative thoughts with some positive retorts.

These strategies will help you tackle the repetitive anxiety loop when it starts up. Simply changing your physical environment or activity can be a powerful distraction technique. Don't let fears or self-doubts get the upper hand. Keep up with the friends, hobbies and interests you had before these troubles started. And mentally responding to anxiety in a new way, with humour or defiance, is also effective. Once you have challenged those negative thoughts once, you are well on your way to beating them.

You may not feel able to cope on your own, which is understandable. Fighting constant depression or anxiety is exhausting so don't feel guilty or ashamed if you need to ask for help. Asking for help is a sign of strength not weakness – because it means you are standing up to the problem and want to deal with it.

Talking to people you trust, perhaps close friends or family, is a good first step. Your GP will be able to offer medical advice and refer you on to a mental health specialist if necessary. (For support with depression, anxiety and OCD, see the further resources at the end of the book.)

However long you have been living with depression, OCD or any form of anxiety disorder, don't despair. A combination of self-help techniques and professional support can be effective. Your mental wellbeing is just as important as your physical wellbeing. It's a cliché but it bears repeating: you wouldn't suffer with a physical illness so why suffer with a mental illness? You're not abnormal and you're not alone. Don't pretend you're OK if you're not. Others have gone through what you are going through and have come out the other side. Many people are there to offer friendship and sympathy, expert support and advice. So be strong and ask for it.

Social media and wellbeing

Addiction

Addiction is the state of being enslaved to a habit or practice or to something that is psychologically or physically habit-forming to such an extent that stopping it causes trauma. It is a dependency, craving, habit, weakness, compulsion, fixation, enslavement.

Are you addicted to your smartphone? Perhaps you think 'addicted' is a bit strong? Sure you use it a lot, you need it for work and for keeping in contact with friends and family. But you're not enslaved or dependent or addicted – of course not. Have you ever mislaid your phone and felt utterly lost? Have you ever felt the panic of watching your battery drain away from 50 per cent to 30 per cent or dashed into a phone shop begging to use their charger? Have you ever felt stressed when there's no Wi-Fi or compulsively checked your screen when the network goes down or seen children go into meltdown when their devices are removed? And when did you last spend a whole day without your phone?

The truth is that we are a lot more dependent than we think. There are around 7.7 billon phone connections in the world, more than there are human beings. Only 14 years after launching, Facebook now has 2 billion active monthly users. That's more than a quarter of the global population, which in 2017 was estimated to have reached 7.6 billion people.

This is a very recent phenomenon. But for children, teens and 20-somethings, so-called digital natives, it is not recent nor even remarkable. Generation Z, also known as the i-Generation (those born from the mid-1990s onwards) have grown up with the internet and have never known a world before smartphones and social media. But in terms of the 6 million-year history of our universe, or even just the past 200,000 years of modern humankind, the digital revolution is a massively new experiment. The World Wide Web is now 29 years old and the internet is 49 years old: in terms of human evolution, this is barely a blink of an eye. The size of this vast 'web' fluctuates, but there are well over 50 billion pages of information, opinion, images, stories, secrets and lies out there, freely available on your smartphone. So it's valid to ask what on earth it's doing to our minds and bodies, our heads and hearts, to our physical and mental wellbeing.

Studies consistently show that we underestimate the amount of hours we spend on our phones. Figures vary, but research conducted by British psychologists found that young adults used their phones an average of five hours a day – approximately one third of their total waking hours. A recent report from the Organisation for Economic Co-operation and Development (OECD) classified 37 per cent of 15-year-olds in the UK as 'extreme internet users'. Another study, using data collected by a screen lock app, estimated that the average user checks their phone around 110 times a day – once every six or seven seconds, with some users unlocking their devices up to 900 times in a single day.

Whether you are in the lower or higher category, it's clear that many of us are online for a significant proportion of the day. We look at our smartphone first thing in the morning and last thing at night. It's our alarm clock, our diary, our contacts book, our photo album, our music player, our mirror and of course our computer. Increasingly, it's our wallet and bank account too, as we scan and pay for things with our phones. It's our A–Z map and satnav when we're in an unfamiliar area. It's our constant companion, a way to pass the time, it's our magazine or book on a long train journey, it's a crutch in social situations, it's our personal publicity tool and source of daily news and instant entertainment rolled into one. It's all these things and more.

But is it also damaging? What is this dependence doing to our mental health and wellbeing?

Many of us feel instinctively that we do spend too much time online, especially on social media. We resent the huge corporations who have sucked us in, targeting us as consumers even if we ignore their fake news and relentless advertising. We realize they must have access to our contacts book – why else are we suddenly connected with old friends we haven't spoken to in years? We know they must be monitoring our searches or why else are we getting pop-ups about those beautiful boots we wanted to buy last week?

When you stop to reflect, it's sinister quite how much they know. In general we dislike being spied on. We dislike being targeted and pro-filed, our personal information sold on to third parties for their relentless marketing campaigns. It's hard to know if anything is private any more, when it seems that everything from our supermarket purchases to our gym attendance to our online dating behaviour is being mined for com-mercial advantage. We simply don't feel comfortable being monitored online: even though we know our emails don't contain state secrets, it still feels intrusive that they are being accessed.

Hence we have a sneaking admiration for people who aren't online, who don't bother posting selfies or pretending their lives are filter-fabulous. Some of the coolest celebrities have opted out of this brave new virtual world. They don't want constant connected-ness. There is a move back to using 'old-school' mobiles, with actual buttons and simple text functions – while others are ditching their phones altogether. Just as it is considered eccentric and therefore hip not to own a smartphone, so it's quirky and cool not to bother with social media. A friend of mine said to me recently: 'I don't actually want to tell everyone where I am and what I'm doing all the time. Is that odd?'

The issue of who owns our personal information online hit the headlines in 2018, with the revelation that the data of up to 90 million Facebook users had been 'improperly shared' with third parties without their knowledge or consent. Facebook's share price dropped and thousands of users deleted their accounts. Hundreds of thousands more decided to check their pages for the first time and tighten up their privacy settings. Like others, I was astonished to find myself linked to hundreds of apps I had never signed up with. Comments such as 'I'm angry at Facebook – but I'm also addicted. How do I break free?' caused wry, anxious smiles in many of us.

This ransacking of our personal data (and that of our friends and contacts) without our consent has definitely dented the image of the smiley Californian company. *The Guardian* newspaper described 'the growing sense that Facebook is all profit and no responsibility.' The scandal continues to unfold – with many other media corporations potentially involved in similar data harvesting and exploitation. This has highlighted how much personal information we unwittingly share without consenting and without understanding the consequences. To Facebook and Twitter and LinkedIn and Instagram and WhatsApp and YouTube and Tumblr we are 'users' – addicted, anyone? Their advertisers are more important than we are: we're just a source of revenue.

Call it paranoia or call it taking responsibility, but it seems we are finally starting to wake up to the vast quantities of personal data swilling around out there in cyberspace. Sadly, it has become safer to assume that no message, purchase, search, personal problem or online interaction is private any more. As the saying goes, if you're not paying for a product, you're the product being sold. We've been using Facebook, Instagram, WhatsApp (the latter two both owned by Facebook) and all the other fun apps for free for years – and now we're paying the price.

Does this affect our wellbeing? Does it matter? Perhaps we have passed the point of no return; perhaps we are too lazy or powerless or addicted to do anything about it. Most of us find ourselves back online the moment our alarm clocks go off – I know I do. We are starting to discover the truth, yet we go on, compulsively scrolling and Googling, uploading and liking, stoking their vast social media enterprises with our thoughts and worries and questions and searches.

Astoundingly, many have introduced yet more monitoring into their personal space, with some 20 million worldwide users of Alexa, Amazon's virtual assistant, which sits in the corner of your home listening to everything you say . . .

With Wi-Fi now all-pervasive, it is no longer a question of logging in, but a question of logging out, consciously opting to disable your digital settings or ditch your smartphone altogether. The line between actuality and virtual reality is so blurred that it can be hard to distinguish between choice, addiction and habit.

> ❛ *Half the time I don't even know why I'm on my phone. Literally it's a reflex action whenever I'm bored; I'll grab my phone and flick through the apps, see if anyone's posted anything, check the weather, Google some celebrity or random event, but I'm rarely looking for anything in particular. Mostly I'm staring at the screen waiting for something to happen, maybe a WhatsApp or a Snapchat to flash up. Or I'll send a silly emoji to a friend for no particular reason. Feels like my brain is sort of fixated and idle at the same time.* ❜ **Jo, 31**

That is exactly what the software designers are aiming for. Their clever, fun, persuasive messaging services are designed in a way to maximize the amount of time we spend inside the app. It's reported that Slack users spend an average of ten hours per day on or actively using the app. Every time we get the ping of an instant message, a speech bubble or a heart-shaped 'like' popping up on our phone, we experience a little rush of dopamine. This isn't hit and miss: the digital overlords have invested billions of dollars into neuroscientific research to improve (in other words, to increase) our User Experience ('UX' is big business).

Like any business their aim is to maximize our usage – but in this case, it infiltrates our entire lives. We are well and truly hooked, with, like Jo in the quote above, our brains 'sort of fixated and idle', physically immobile but mentally immersed in a virtual world that – lest we forget – is not real.

The lost art of concentration

It's not all fun and games. We underestimate just how relentless and demanding the constant onslaught of communication can be. Social media and constant messaging can seriously affect our intellectual wellbeing. It can prevent us from reaching our full potential, both professionally and personally. That may sound dramatic but it's true: the sheer volume of mini-chats, pictures, messages, posts and texts can wreak havoc on our concentration and productivity levels. Real-time chat apps may be less intrusive than phone calls, because in theory we can respond when we are ready, but this rarely happens. Usually, if we are working or studying and any message pops up, we will check it immediately. Then we reply, then they reply, then we reply . . . and so on. We are caught in a constant loop of communication, often with five or ten different chats going on at once.

Is it any wonder we find it hard to concentrate on the task in front of us? As Gloria Mark, an expert in 'interruption science', explains, the distraction factor is considerable: 'The average knowledge worker switches tasks every three minutes, and, once distracted, a worker takes nearly a half-hour to resume the original task.'

Think hard about the interruptions from your smartphone and what impact these might be having on your own productivity. Being honest, I know that my productivity suffers. I know that on the rare occasions when I am away from my phone – when I am offline and physically separated from any form of direct or indirect messaging – I get far more work done. My mind is clearer and my thoughts are more focused. I have original ideas and follow them through, rather than Googling facts online, getting sucked into cyberspace and losing my thread.

Think about how much more you could accomplish if you were fully focused on the work in front of you. It might be A levels, revision for your university degree, the first chapter of a novel, your PhD thesis, a business plan, a conference paper or a work report. Without any interruptions from your smartphone you're guaranteed to do it better and faster. Your career or academic progress will benefit. Your concentration and productivity will improve. Isn't that worth more than the dopamine rush of yet another WhatsApp?

Phone-phobia

There may be plenty of interaction going on, but not very much talking. Anything too real scares us, as Jo continues:

> ❛ I can't cope with phone calls though. Unscheduled calls just freak me out. Texts and WhatsApps and emails are fine but if someone starts ringing it feels too immediate, almost intrusive. I never just call people out of the blue, if I do I text them first and have to mentally prepare for full-on conversation. I sometimes text my sister and tell her I'm going to call and can we leave voicemails. ❜

Jo is not alone in dodging real live phone calls. More and more people consider a ringing phone a form of ambush. Calling someone out of the blue can feel presumptuous or 'intrusive' – who knows what they're doing? Over a quarter of adults never use their smartphones to make calls. We have developed phone avoidance or even phone-phobia, opting instead for indirect methods of human contact. Messaging services are direct and instantaneous but they allow us to respond when we are ready, giving us time to think about and craft a response. We're in constant communication but we can maintain the illusion of control.

Telephone conversations, on the other hand, demand tricky things such as spontaneity and improvisation. And then there's the stress of saying goodbye: how do you conclude a conversation without peak awkwardness? It's no wonder we get anxious.

However daunting it feels, talking is good for our emotional wellbeing. Back in the 1990s an advertising slogan from British Telecom reminded us, 'It's good to talk' – and that still holds true today. Many developmental psychologists are warning that a generation are growing up without the art of conversation. Emojis and tweets and hashtags are expressive in their own way, but they leave out an entire dimension of interpersonal skills that real life interaction demands.

Remember the real world

It's not only human conversations that are being affected by our smartphone dependence. Think about the real world around you and what you are missing out on. When did you last spend a bus journey sitting on the top deck, gazing out at the busy streets below? When did you last sit in a café alone, just people-watching? When did you last sit down with pen and paper and write a letter or send a postcard? When did you last catch someone's eye on the train and strike up a conversation? When did you last eavesdrop on strangers or notice a funny street sign or even get talking to the cashier in the supermarket?

We risk losing all these human moments of connection when we are glued to our screens, compulsively texting or tweeting, or talking into Alexa-style virtual assistants in our own homes. We miss out on the randomness and the unexpected when we confine ourselves to the digital universe. Although we may be 'connecting' with billions of users across the world, we are not interacting with the people around us. Our digital devices have, in some sense, hijacked our physical lives.

And then there's the psychological aspect. What is social media actually doing to us? What's it doing to you? How does it affect your self-esteem, your relationships, your energy levels, your concentration, your view of the world?

I'll be there for you

Loyalty, understanding, empathy, openness, trust, honesty, acceptance, respect . . . These were the qualities mentioned by almost every person when I asked what they look for in their friends. It's no surprise we all value these qualities: they are the basis on which true friendship is founded. But does digital communication destroy all this?

Whether you view technology as positive or negative for human relationships, it has increased overall levels of communication, albeit through diverse channels. According to a recent Facebook study, the top five forms of communication are now messaging (67 per cent), social media (48 per cent), email (47 per cent), video chat (47 per cent) and face to face (38 per cent). As these modes of communication have proliferated, users report greater social satisfaction and more frequent and authentic conversations in real life too.

This can be hard to square with the loneliness findings outlined in Chapter 7, Relationships, but perhaps both can be true. Every one of us can make our relationships more meaningful simply by making time to connect, sending that text or postcard or email, picking up the phone or dropping round for a visit. True human connection is about communication, about caring what's really happening in each other's lives, not about the perfect selfie you posted that morning. True friends can see behind the façade and the filters; they can sense when you're feeling sad.

One-to-one

Then there are our intimate relationships, those exclusive partnerships we form with one special other, as boyfriend, girlfriend, partner, husband or wife. These private relationships have also been revolutionized by digital communication and not always in a good way. All too often texts and emails cause misunderstandings because they lack tone and context. Just as with friends, it is important to sustain genuine human contact, both verbal and physical. If you and your partner live apart or are in a long-distance relationship, make time to speak on the phone. If you are travelling for work, stay in touch. Take five minutes to share breakfast or have dinner dates over Skype. Even if you live together, remember the importance of being physically present for each other. No matter how busy life gets, you can always switch off your devices and talk together at the end of the day.

Communication and wellbeing

The modern cliché – that social media is having the effect of bringing us all closer together – is not always true. Superficial connections on social media can make us feel more, not less, lonely. At times it can seem as though everyone else is out there at parties, on Ayurvedic retreats or glamorous work trips, having perfect relationships and busy successful careers, and we are all alone, at home, missing out. Online communication can be a wedge as well as a bridge.

The 'instant' nature of twenty-first-century communication can affect your wellbeing. The 'instant' part is possible in theory but it is not always the reality. Just because we can all reply to everything instantly, it does not mean that we do. In pre-digital times you might send a letter and then wait patiently for a response, but you couldn't expect to hear back immediately. You wouldn't sit there staring at your device, fretting over the wording, wondering if you'd said something wrong, wishing you could un-send it, constantly refreshing the screen and waiting desperately for a reply. You wouldn't then stalk the recipient online, monitoring their status updates and wondering why if they can post GIFs of cats, they can't reply to your WhatsApp. (OK, you might sit by the landline or letterbox instead!)

There is nothing louder than the sound of a phone not ringing – or your notification not pinging. Instantaneous is problematic: the moment you hit send you know the message has arrived, but then the agony of waiting and worrying begins. It is all speeded up, with barely any time to reflect or anticipate: as soon as you have said 'your bit' you are waiting for 'their bit'.

We have probably all had the experience of working ourselves up into a state over nothing: convinced that someone is ignoring you when in fact they are going through a busy period. Maybe they want to take time to write you a proper reply. Maybe they are ill or having a family crisis. Maybe they just forgot. Rationally, we know there are many reasons why they might not have replied yet – but it doesn't stop us from getting paranoid! We invent all sorts of emotional tensions with people who aren't experiencing them back.

Twitter, Facebook and Instagram can exacerbate anxiety and neurosis too, especially when you post something and get absolutely no response. Not a single comment, no likes or heart emojis or thumbs up. Everyone thinks you're worthless, not worth a single click? Even worse, you post something and start getting unfollowed . . . so now you are not just ignorable, you are actually repellent? It is easy to get caught up in these cycles of self-flagellation, especially if you are already feeling vulnerable. Social media can intensify existing feelings of isolation and anxiety.

The potential for instant messaging to cause social embarrassment is also considerable. If a professional contact hasn't responded to an email you sent weeks ago, should you resend it? If a good friend hasn't replied to the text, should you badger them? What about in a new relationship, is it OK to send several messages in a row or are you coming across like a stalker? It's a minefield of awkwardness.

This is not to condemn all forms of digital interaction. Recent surveys report that up to 80 per cent of adults and over 90 per cent of teenagers message every day. Even if we are not addicted, we definitely love our endless messaging. If we can rein in our expectations, they mostly work well.

WhatsApps and texts and emails and tweets are quick, cheap and easy; they have added a new dimension to human intercourse and they are enjoyable daily distractions. We now have more frequent contact with friends and family than ever before, with even elderly relatives getting in on the action (my godmother, in her mid-eighties, is on WhatsApp!). If we can keep things in perspective, not catastrophize about being ignored on social media, not overreact when we don't receive instant replies to our instant messages, technology really can bring us closer together.

But nothing replaces human interaction IRL: an hour in a café over coffee and cake with a friend, say, or great conversation over dinner. In modern life we don't have much spare time for regular get-togethers, but when we make the effort it's worth a million Facebook 'likes'.

Social media and your wellbeing

As we have seen, interaction with other human beings is a Good Thing – but how does social media specifically affect our wellbeing? As I mentioned, the World Wide Web has been with us for less than 30 years, and Facebook for less than 15 years, compared with mankind's 200,000 years of civilization. This timespan matters, because it reminds us of what we are designed to cope with, in an evolutionary sense. Of course the human species is flexible and able to adapt to our changing climate and environment. It is impossible to predict the future and who knows how our brains will gradually evolve to cope with digitization: perhaps artificial intelligence will take over thinking and working for us entirely one day.

But for now at least we are still human beings with physical bodies designed to run, jump, touch and play. We are social animals, we gather in groups, whether that's couples, families, friendship circles or communities. Traditionally, human beings communicate a lot, talking and touching each other. We create new human beings through the most intimate form of contact, love-making. We express our emotions, both negative and positive, through fighting or embracing, enmity or friendship, war or peace. Interaction with other humans, both verbal and actual, is our norm. Perhaps it's unsurprising that the purely textual, virtual or digital interaction online leaves us feeling isolated and depressed.

You can minimize the depressive effects of social media by thinking carefully about what you follow. As I mentioned in Chapter 2, Mood, confidence and self-esteem, a while ago I unfollowed quite a few of the 'fitspo' brigade on social media. Their perfectly pure, plant-based, gym-obsessed clean living was filling my timeline and, you know what, it was getting me down! The endless Instagrams of their raw-food diets and training regimes were incredibly unhelpful for me, like a morning dose of self-recrimination: I'd feel guilty for not being at a spinning class at the gym or greedy for eating actual real food as opposed to a glass of spirulina and spinach.

This is not to say that social media is always a negative influence – far from it. There are plenty of brilliant health and wellness accounts out there, for example from inspiring women who may have suffered from poor body image or disordered eating in the past and have chosen to open up about their struggles. Some have recovered, others are recovering, vlogging their experiences along the way, offering advice and inspiring others.

This kind of supportive community is social media at its best, because the honesty we can share online can be wonderful, but we need to choose our influences carefully. Instinct is a good rule of thumb, so trust your feelings. If someone is consistently making you feel inadequate or insecure, if their posts make you feel guilty or greedy, unfollow them.

A female friend recently posted:

> ❝ Instagram can have so much power and influence over our recovery, our mood and what we choose to eat next. It's kind of up to us how we use the eating disorder recovery community and whether we choose to follow things that keep us focused on illness or those which inspire us with wellness. I think it's important to keep a cool and positive social media network. ❞

Another replied:

> ❝ Yes – and in recovery, unfollowing people isn't a criticism against them, but just that I can't "do" their content at that particular time. It's hard for me to hit that unfollow button because I'm anxious dealing with any aftermath. But it's my recovery at the end of the day, so if stuff hurts me, it needs to go for a while and that needs to be OK to do. ❞

Their exchange highlights the positive aspects of recovery communities on social media, in which one can share and draw inspiration and support from like-minded friends, but also the potential downsides. We have to be resilient, we have to look after ourselves and our mental health, especially when it's fragile, as in recovery. Following unhelpful influences can trigger further guilt and disordered eating – and even unfollowing others can be fraught with anxiety.

This post was accompanied by a plate of cheeringly indulgent chocolate brownies, however, which I think we can all endorse.

Social media: a tool or a trap?

Of course there are both advantages and benefits: many of us have a love–hate relationship with social media. We admit that we are too dependent on it, that we waste hours unhealthily snooping into other people's online lives and that it sometimes makes us feel terrible about ourselves . . . yet it's hard to disconnect. It affects us in different ways, depending on our personal issues, our interests and who we follow. Here are a few more frank confessions from readers!

> ❛ I have mixed opinions . . . I like that social media lets me talk to others in the same boat and reminds me that I'm not alone. It keeps me connected to the outside world on days where my depression is a weight on my shoulders and I struggle to leave the house. Sometimes I feel I need to disconnect from social media and I think it would help – but I know I can't, I'd be leaving a world behind. ❜ **Gemma, 21**

> ❛ Social media is a massive part of anxiety and depression. That constant feeling of missing out can be overwhelming. You can easily forget that people only post about the times when they're out having fun, not when they're sitting at home alone. This can lead me to feeling anxious and lonely – and I'm 29; I can only imagine how hard it is to be a teenager now, that constant feeling of anxiety could easily lead to depression. Social media can also lead to your emotions being dependent on

what other people are doing. You see something you don't want to see and bang, your day is ruined out of the blue. **Emma, 29**

I'd say social media is both good and bad, it has ruined a lot of things and helped a lot of things. I use it a lot, Facebook, Instagram, Twitter, Snapchat, etc. . . . so I don't hate it enough to stop using it. I do sometimes feel like I need to come off Instagram as there are lots of accounts promoting eating disorders. I feel like they 100 per cent need to be taken down . . . **Ellie, 17**

I feel I'm dependent on social media and without it I would feel very isolated. However it is definitely a contributing factor to mental illness with all the triggering content and also the lack of personal interaction. **Sophie, 19**

Helping with isolation is clearly one of the positive aspects of social media. And it can be harmless fun, a way of relaxing and unwinding, a bit of time wasting on Instagram, posting your selfies with friends. These women also highlight the downsides, however. The sheer ubiquity of social media, the fact that many of us are constantly online, anxiously checking and comparing ourselves with others, means that it can be yet another source of worry and it really does have an impact on our mental health and wellbeing.

In vulnerable individuals, those who are already feeling anxious or depressed, it can even pose a threat. Remember those NHS findings that over one quarter of young women are now suffering common mental health symptoms such as anxiety, panic and depression. Health officials said they were particularly concerned about the trends in the youngest age group, those aged 16–24 who are growing up in the era of social media.

The statistics are alarming. In 1993 young women were twice as likely as young men to exhibit common mental health symptoms, but they are now three times more likely to experience them. Again, this has been attributed to the prevalence of social media, with young women thought to be more vulnerable than men.

The thief of joy

In an ideal world, we would use social media only for support and inspiration, rather than self-flagellation and comparison. We would enjoy the positive aspects and avoid the negative ones. But unfortunately it's not that simple.

You may know the saying, 'comparison is the thief of joy' – and it's true. The moment we start measuring ourselves against others we fall short. Comparing your life with that of others will only bring you down. How many times have you felt satisfied with a personal achievement, then realized other people are doing much better? I've often felt proud of a book, say, and then realized other authors are selling 10 or 20 times as many copies!

This is the classic compare-and-despair syndrome. On social media we get other people's highlights reel, while all around us is our own messy, chaotic behind-the-scenes reality. Their flawless photos make us feel ugly, their rigorous workouts make us feel lazy, their clean eating makes us feel fat and greedy, their sparkling professional success makes us feel like failures. Something that should unite us, this digital sharing of our thoughts and images of our lives together, can make us feel intensely sad and alone.

This sense of loneliness or inadequacy is widespread and explains those rising levels of anxiety and depression (particularly among young women, the heaviest social media users). Given that we are spending hours every day online, isn't it worth reflecting on what it's doing to our self-esteem, our emotional and mental wellbeing?

Here are some reflections from others that might resonate with you.

> ❝ Social media is toxic to the mind and unfortunately very addictive. I use it far too much and have definitely noticed a decline in my mental wellbeing because of it. I always end up seeing something I didn't want to see or being triggered by these luxurious lives people are pretending to live through their photos. ❞ **Taylor, 19**

❢ *I have a love–hate relationship with social media . . . through making modifications to it I feel it's finally loosening its grip on me. I only use Facebook for messaging people and have blocked the newsfeed. I use Instagram but I don't follow people who might make me feel guilty about my life and food choices, and I use Twitter for work. I'm a bit of a phone addict but I regularly take breaks from social media.* ❣
Letty, 29

Selfie-mania

I was amazed recently when a friend casually mentioned that she was tagged in 'over 10,000 photos' on Facebook. She is in her early twenties, a true digital native, and social media is as natural to her as photo albums were to older people in the past. But still, 10,000 photos? It seems like a heck of a lot of your private life made public!

Those distinctions between private and public are becoming blurred, some would say irrelevant. It's now completely normal to share photos from the bathroom or bedroom, in your underwear or pyjamas, sleepy selfies from the depths of your own duvet, even 'snuggling' with your partner in bed.

It's cool to post selfies of oneself au naturel, looking 'undone' but also flawless, thus demonstrating one's inner beauty. Embracing the imperfectly perfect movement, messy bed-hair and all, while actually looking pretty darn perfect. Beauty bloggers and celebrities have leapt on the no-make-up trend with enthusiasm, although one suspects that some of them take quite a while finessing their make-up-free selfies. Don't believe the #nofilter hype – to borrow from a Dolly Parton phrase, it takes a lot of work to look this natural!

The whole social media scene can be confusing and also weirdly dishonest. The important thing is not to be seen to be trying too hard, not to reveal how much you care what others think, never to make too much of an effort. It's like claiming you 'just threw this old thing on' after spending hours planning your outfit. Celebrities like Jennifer

Lawrence, Cara Delevingne and Katy Perry embody this casual tomboy perfection, appearing never to give a damn, working an old pair of boyfriend jeans and still looking glamorous or a couture dress on the red carpet with trainers, covered in tattoos but with immaculate make-up and the correct proportion of multiple piercings.

For those of us mere mortals without stylists and make-up artists and social media managers it can be hard to measure up. When we are unhappy with our weight, desperate to exercise off the flab or starve ourselves down to the ideal body shape, trying to portray our best selves online, it is easy to become depressed and anxious and to feel alone.

The FaceTune app, which enables users to digitally retouch their selfies, has been a runaway success. With self-editing features such as the 'heal' button to get rid of blemishes and the 'smooth' tool to even out enlarged pores, FaceTune has sold more than 10 million copies, and was Apple's most popular app of 2017.

But what's all this self-editing and digital altering doing to us? Should we really be gazing at and trying to perfect our own images for hours every day? Is it any coincidence that the word for our most narcissistic daily creations, selfies, is so close to selfish?! As well as creating anxiety and dissatisfaction when we compare ourselves to others, social media overload can also make us rather selfish.

Social scientists have noted a correlation between the rise of the selfie and a decline in altruism. When the camera was first invented, taking photographs was about looking outwards, capturing a beautiful view, iconic landmark or a gathering of loved ones. Now the camera is firmly trained on the taker, putting the individual at the centre of everything. Of course, there's a time and a place for including oneself in a scene or taking group photos, but we should beware of the selfie craze tipping into self-obsession.

The TV presenter Claudia Winkleman deleted her Instagram app. In her *Sunday Times* column she admitted: 'instead of living, I was watching other people living. And worse, they were stopping what they were doing and capturing and sharing instead of living it, too.'

Then of course there's the notorious 'humblebrag', otherwise known as false humility or self-deprecatingly telling the world how great you are and how much you are winning at life. 'So I got this so-and-so award – obviously they made a mistake!' is a perfect example of the humblebrag.

Whether it's selfies, Instastories or humblebragging, this stuff is time-consuming and inwardly focused – it does our emotional well-being no favours. Rather than experiencing the world around us – the sunrise over the desert or the romantic evening with your partner – you are taking and retaking the shot, trying to capture the best angle, inserting yourself into it, worrying about your hair or adjusting the filters. Too often when we are trying to capture these 'perfect' images from behind our phones, the stylish plate of food or that artfully swirled cup of coffee, we miss the moment itself. Who are we trying to impress? Does anyone really care? Why not drink the coffee while it's hot instead!

How to disconnect

From personal experience I would say that taking regular breaks from social media is the single best thing you can do for your mental health and wellbeing. Being online simply eats up too much potential time and emotional energy that could be used for other things, whether that's work, relationship or personal goals. When we don't pursue our ambitions, when we find ourselves trapped and addicted to our devices, our mood and self-esteem actually suffers. I know this feeling: I look at other people's amazing achievements – a marathon they've signed up for, a three-book publishing deal, a clothing line they've launched – and I think, why not me? What have I been doing while they've been out there achieving so much? The answer is often that we have been wasting our time online, mindlessly scrolling, observing, comparing.

And what about resolutions and targets? Many of our best intentions – learning a new skill, spending more time with friends or family, sorting out the garden or just getting more sleep – are derailed by the temptations of our gadgets. The constant distraction they provide is unlike anything humans have known before. Unlike going to the cinema, shopping or any other leisure activity that still requires a certain degree of patience, we don't need to wait: the online distractions contained within our phones are always available. You can watch, discuss, check or buy almost anything, anytime, right there on your screen. You can go weeks without speaking to another person or leaving the house.

This is a practical problem – we're surrounded by connectivity – but there are practical solutions.

- **Disable notifications** Receiving alerts continually wreaks havoc with your concentration. You don't need the 'ping' every time a message arrives.
- **Remove yourself physically from the distracting device** Put your phone in a drawer in another room.
- **Don't use your phone as an alarm** It's the first thing you see on waking and, before you know it, you're online, checking emails, updating Twitter, posting on Instagram and you've blown the mental morning clarity. Don't go on social media at the start of the day: your personal goals must come first.
- **Ban phones from the table** Agree with your family and friends that you won't bring gadgets to mealtimes. This frees you up to focus on tasting and enjoying the food, digesting it well and being present to interact with others. Do the same when eating alone.
- **Take it slow** If a phone detox day feels too much (or is impractical), start with a regular detox hour. Allocate just 60 minutes a day to unplugging and doing something REAL: read the newspaper, listen to a new album, bake some bread, potter around the garden. Imagine if you took just an hour of that wasted online time, every day and dedicated it to working towards your dream . . .

Remember, you don't have to go cold turkey. Depending on your work schedule and personal preferences, you can just start with disconnecting for 30 minutes or an hour. Gradually you can extend this . . . and notice how your wellbeing improves!

Our digital dependence can be detrimental to our wellbeing and can hold us back more than we realize.

Bedroom blackout

We all have different tolerance levels for technology and some of us are more prone to that feeling of brain-fuddling digital overload than others. I urge you to keep your bedroom technology-free, however. As explored in Chapter 3, Depression, anxiety and obsessive-compulsive disorders, digital devices really are not conducive to rest, relaxation or sleep. Your bedroom should be more cave and less multimedia centre! If you don't like the idea of a cave, think darkened sanctuary or candlelit spa instead.

Many smartphones, laptops and TVs emit blue light, a short-wavelength light that disrupts our body's natural production of melatonin. When we stare at bright screens for prolonged periods, levels of this essential sleep hormone are reduced by around a quarter. Even a quick glance at the screen during the night can seriously interfere with our sleep cycle. If you need more motivation (more reasons?) to keep those devices out of your bedroom, and for more information on sleeping well, see Chapter 8, Sleep.

Back to reality

We can't un-invent the internet, nor would most of us want to. Like others, I enjoy social media for the variety, companionship and enter-tainment it provides. And the progress brought about by the digital revolution has been profound, in everything from scientific break-throughs to global democracy to our working lives and social networks. But technology can also be distracting and dehumanizing.

If we focus on work when we are working, we will in the long term be more productive and fulfilled individuals, with more time for real human interaction. Chatting online has been compared with junk food: addictive and moreish but ultimately unsatisfying. Getting that work–social–digital balance right has never been more important, as smartphones creep into every corner of our lives. Reclaiming our brains for uninterrupted work or study, being able to concentrate on a book or a film or music and genuine human contact are more beneficial for our wellbeing than superficial junk food interaction.

We must be aware of how technology is swallowing up more and more of our waking hours. We must recognize when social media and 24/7 connectedness are affecting our wellbeing. We must be vigilant about our physical and mental health. Above all, we need to take back control, harnessing technology for positive ends in our own lives and tackling the negative aspects.

Be honest with yourself about how much time you're spending online. Examine your digital behaviour: is it enjoyable or addictive? If social media is making you anxious or exacerbating your depression, if you're comparing yourself with others and feeling low, if you're being triggered or influenced by unhealthy lifestyle messages – take a break! Unfollow or mute or simply delete the app. It really is that simple.

Try disconnecting and see whether it makes a difference. You may, like me, enjoy regular digital detoxes or have the occasional unplugged weekend or even decide to come off social media altogether. Stay self-aware; be curious about the world around you. Distinguish between the digital world and the living, breathing world – your family and friends, your pets, wildlife and nature all around you. Write a letter or a card to someone you love. Use your smartphone for something really smart: an actual phone call. Prioritize real experiences over virtual, make time for human interaction in real life. By all means embrace this brave new world, but don't let it get you down.

5

Nutrition, diet and wellbeing

A well-known reality TV star extolling her extreme juice diet posted, 'After 21 days of juicing I've lost 1 stone 4 lbs. I feel detoxed, cleansed within like I couldn't be healthier, my anxiety and tiredness is non-existent . . .'

As anyone who has been on a diet will know, food has a noticeable impact on our wellbeing. When we restrict, radically alter or go without food, we do not just get hungry, we also get low – because food is more than just fuel. It is essential to our physical survival but it is also an integral part of who we are as humans, how we live, how we feel about ourselves and what we care about.

Think about your personal eating, shopping and cooking habits: how do they reflect your personality? Maybe you are a passionate foodie who loves trying out the latest restaurant. Or maybe you are a skilled amateur chef who is always in the kitchen experimenting with new recipes. Do you grab a sandwich on the go and usually eat while walking, talking, working or on the phone? Or do you treat mealtimes as sacrosanct and always plate up your food, lay the table and use proper cutlery? Do you pore over cookery books and websites or flick straight past the food supplements in your Sunday newspaper? Is your kitchen the most important room in your house or just a place to boil the kettle? Are you curious and adventurous about trying foreign cuisine when travelling or wary of strange grub, preferring to stick with familiar favourites? Do you have special dietary restrictions or allergies or will you eat pretty much anything going? Do you identify with a tribe: are you vegan, Paleo or a 'clean eater'? Do you worry about intensive farming, animal welfare and the environment? Do you shop and eat seasonally or just whatever takes your fancy? Do you judge others on their choices or never even notice what other people eat?

Clearly, our attitudes to food say a lot about us and that's before we even get into the realm of bodies and weight and emotions. It's no wonder we find it fascinating to peer into the contents of someone else's fridge.

Everything about our individual nutrition habits is revealing, including how and where and when we shop. These days the options are endless: we can order online from all the big supermarkets, we can source specialist ingredients from every corner of the globe, we can buy local at our artisan bakery and posh butcher or pop round to the corner shop or even drive to a 24-hour supermarket at midnight. Some people rarely shop at all and simply order their meals in from the many bike delivery services available.

Then there's how much we spend on food: some people splurge a good proportion of their income on dining out (or ordering in), while others stick to a strict food budget. Some stock up on economy own-brands while others pay twice the price for premium products. Your shopping basket can be as revealing as your fridge: would you feed your kids frozen fish fingers; is your milk organic; is your coffee and chocolate Fair Trade; do you buy single mini-bottles of wine for one; do you hide the crisps under the virtuous bag of spinach? Do you shun plastic packaging and only shop at eco-friendly stores? Is everything in your basket grass-fed, cage-free and wild?

Clearly, what we eat is about more than just the size of our jeans, our body mass index (BMI) or the number on the bathroom scales. Our food attitudes and behaviour reveal much about our personalities and priorities, our homes and our family, our income and our social life, our morals and our manners, our values and our neuroses, our quirks and our childhoods, our relationships, ethnicity, culture and memories.

Whether it's fermenting our own kimchi, cutting out gluten, liquidizing our breakfast into a raw power juice or Instagramming a picture of our dinner, no other species has evolved such complicated social and emotional rituals around the business of eating. We put vast quantities of time and money into acquiring, preparing and consuming our food. We spend a lot of time alternately treating and depriving ourselves. We spend a lot of time worrying about our dietary choices – and, hopefully still, a lot of time thinking about what we're going to eat next.

Before all that . . .

Before we get into the complicated emotions, morals, habits and rituals that surround eating, let's remind ourselves of the facts. You may know Virginia Woolf's oft-quoted words: 'One cannot think well, love well, sleep well, if one has not dined well.' This line (from her 1929 essay *A Room of One's Own*) captures perfectly the role of food in our body's basic functioning. Food is fundamental to how our body operates: we get out what we put in. Without good food we will not be able to think clearly, sleep deeply or love well!

We often get so caught up in the weight gain and weight loss issues that we forget what else food does. When we restrict calories, skip meals or opt for synthetic low-fat choices, we are depriving our bodies of essential nutrients. More importantly, we are also depriving our brain. The brain is the body's hungriest organ, consuming up to 20 per cent of our daily caloric intake even at rest (and a bit more when we are working or studying hard). This is because your brain needs energy, in the form of glucose, to produce and release chemical signals called neurotransmitters to facilitate its many different cognitive functions. Without a regular caloric intake it is hard to concentrate or study or even think straight; when you are hungry you may become irritable and distracted. A malnourished body is a malnourished brain.

'You are what you eat' is a familiar saying. It is also a valuable reminder that the foods we eat are the building blocks from which our cells are made, renewed and repaired. Returning to the car analogy (see Chapter 1, Body image and wellbeing), you expect to put high-quality fuel into a high-performance machine. The more nutritious the food we consume, the better our personal machines will operate. Good food gives us energy, strengthens our muscles and bones, bolsters our immune system against illnesses and disease, even protects against dementia. Good grub is also essential for clear skin, sparkling eyes and glossy hair!

Specific foods have been shown to be particularly beneficial for optimum brain functioning, while others appear to be particularly detrimental. Some of the best brain foods include the following.

- **Fatty acids** The brain loves polyunsaturated long-chain and omega-3 fatty acids, especially those found in wild salmon, mackerel, anchovies and sardines, as well as walnuts, flaxseeds and grass-fed meat. Omega-3-rich foods lower cholesterol and blood pressure, strengthen the immune system, boost the health of the brain, joints, heart and eyes and reduce inflammation.

- **Glucose** This is a specific kind of carbohydrate and the only energy source for the brain. We get most of it from foods containing carbohydrates or sugar, such as cereals, bread and pasta – wholemeal products are healthier than ones made with white flour. Other good, healthy sources if you need a boost include legumes, some vegetables, such as potatoes, beetroot, sweet potatoes, onions and spring onions, fruit such as kiwi fruit and grapes, raw honey, maple syrup and coconut sugar.

- **Vitamins and minerals** These are essential for a healthy nervous system and immune system, for fighting infection and disease, for healthy bones and for many other aspects of health. Vitamin A, vitamin C, vitamin E and selenium have an important antioxidant effect, helping to protect us against heart disease and cancer among others. Vitamin E has also been shown to protect against dementia, especially when combined with vitamin C. Iron, copper and zinc are involved in healthy blood vessels, wound healing and ensuring you don't get anaemic. Fruit and vegetables are the best natural sources of vitamins and minerals. Berries, oranges, grapefruit and apples are excellent brain foods, as are leafy green vegetables such as broccoli, cabbage, spinach, kale and dandelion greens. Onions, carrots, tomatoes, squash and nuts also go on this list.

- **Extra-virgin olive oil** This contains high levels of anti-ageing nutrients, such as omega-3s and vitamin E.

These foods all get the green light, but then there's the red light bad brain fuel. The worst are processed foods or those containing 'trans' fats, which increase levels of the unhealthy form of cholesterol. Studies have shown that eating fried and fatty foods regularly increases the risk of cognitive decline and dementia: this damaging effect starts from as little as 2 grams of trans fats a day. Foods to avoid include fried food, such as fish and chips, fatty foods, such as red meat and pork, and baked goods containing trans fats and refined sugar, such as cakes, biscuits, crisps, ready meals, frozen pizza and burgers. Also unhealthy are margarine and processed cheeses, spreadable or 'creamy' products and processed meat such as bacon, salami, ham and hot dogs.

(Incidentally, the scientific evidence for the links between processed meats and cancer is becoming overwhelming. One expert recently called bacon 'the most dangerous food on the planet'.)

Debunking the diet myths

Eating a plentiful range of fresh, nutritious food is clearly beneficial for our physical and mental wellbeing. Moderation, variety and adequate calorie intake are simple, sensible principles and they should be easy to follow. Yet many of us are still seduced by the latest diet myths, sucked into believing that eating 'clean' or 'intermittently' or 'intuitively' holds the key to attaining that super-slim physique, perfect body image, ideal BMI, radiant skin, age-reversing vitality and so on . . . Whether it's novelty, curiosity or yet another celebrity endorsement, it is surprising how easily we are persuaded to buy or try something new by all manner of nutritional nonsense.

Most food fads involve restriction and deprivation, which lead to dietary deficiencies, anxiety and guilt. Here are some of the worst culprits – and good reasons to avoid them!

Low-fat products

This has been a popular weight loss strategy for decades, but increasing evidence shows that eating fat does not make you fat. In fact, the right fats are vital for our health. Eating good, or 'essential', fats is excellent for overall energy levels, mental wellbeing, physical strength and fitness. Fat deficiency leads to a host of problems, including low mood, anxiety and depression, low energy and libido, and poor skin, hair and nails. Insufficient fat intake also prevents the absorption of the fat-soluble vitamins and minerals that are essential for health.

Our mental wellbeing is particularly dependent on a steady supply of good fats. As we have already seen, essential fatty acids are crucial for optimum brain functioning – they help us to learn, concentrate, work, focus and communicate – and the body cannot manufacture these essential fatty acids. As anyone who has tried eating a low-fat or no-fat diet will know, a lack of dietary fat often causes depressed mood. Our emotional stability, sex drive and sleep are also badly affected by low-fat diets. In addition, many 'diet' or fat-free foods are high in artificial sweeteners to compensate for the lack of natural flavour.

Fat doesn't make you fat, so reject the myth that you will lose body fat by cutting back on dietary fat. Instead, reduce the empty nutritional calories in your diet (such as sugar and alcohol) and increase the good fats. Load up on avocados, nuts and oily fish to improve your mood and supercharge your brain.

A gluten-free diet

The gluten-free movement has exploded in recent years, but it is based on seriously shaky nutritional claims. All over the UK people believe that they are allergic to certain foods, the most commonly cited culprit being wheat, hence the demonization of gluten. More than 1 in 5 people in the UK claims to have a food allergy or intolerance, an increase of 400 per cent in the past 20 years. However, research conducted by the University of Portsmouth has shown that of all those claiming to have an allergy or intolerance, only 2 per cent actually do.

Genuine gluten intolerance is serious but rare: only around 1 per cent of the population are thought to suffer from coeliac disease. When susceptible people with this severe form of gluten sensitivity eat gluten it causes the body to mount a strong but misguided immune response, attacking itself by mistake and producing the symptoms of coeliac disease. In the tiny proportion of those with this serious digestive disorder, eating gluten can cause inflammation, abdominal pain and bloating, as well as damage to the small intestine and an inability to absorb nutrients. For people with coeliac disease, avoiding gluten is essential.

However, many gluten-free eaters have self-diagnosed their gluten intolerance on the basis of vague symptoms such as bloating, constipation or diarrhoea. Even commercial tests are unreliable and inaccurate. When questioned, most consumers do not actually know what gluten is or what it does – it is a protein found in wheat, rye and barley that is responsible for the consistency we want in foods made from these grains.

But far from being healthier, gluten-free products may be full of other 'nasties': gluten-free bread, biscuits and cereal, for example, often contain refined ingredients such as additives, flavourings, stabilizers, added sugar and preservatives. Eliminating all wheat from the diet carries the additional risk of consuming insufficient fibre, which can exacerbate digestive problems such as constipation and bloating. A study by the University of Hertfordshire found that, on average, gluten-free alternatives contain more fat, sugar and salt than their natural versions, and thus increase the risk of weight gain. And when you consider that these products can cost up to five times as much as regular versions, gluten-free makes even less sense. In the absence of a medically diagnosed intolerance, it is not necessary to avoid gluten. Instead, why not include more naturally gluten-free alternatives such as brown rice and quinoa?

Dairy-free foods

Dairy products such as milk, yogurt and cheese are an excellent source of calcium and protein, essential for strong bones and teeth. However, many dieters avoid dairy in the quest for weight loss. An estimated 1 in 6 teenagers have cut dairy out of their diet – at a crucial stage of their life for bone building: the latest UK National Diet and Nutrition Survey found that 25 per cent of young women aged 11–18 years are at risk of calcium deficiency due to a low intake of milk.

While vegetables such as spinach and broccoli do contain calcium, dairy products are by far the richest and most easily absorbed sources of this vital nutrient. Milk also provides magnesium, potassium, selenium, zinc, vitamin A, several B vitamins, a small amount of vitamin E and protein. At any age, a dairy-free diet carries the risk of calcium deficiency and reduced bone density, with an increased risk of osteoporosis and osteoarthritis.

Juicing

Like many other 'clean eating' trends, juicing has become wildly popular in recent years. It is especially prevalent on social media: Instagram is awash with vibrant orange and supergreen juices, as well as fresh fruit and vegetables glowing with dietary virtue and promising detox miracles (see Detoxing, below).

Fans of juicing claim that it reduces stress on the digestive system, but in fact the opposite may be true. The body is specifically designed to break down our food – but it needs something solid to break down!

The digestive system is a complex mechanism and it is there for a reason: to extract the nutrients and energy from the food we eat and get rid of what we don't need. In order to function optimally, our intestines need fibre and bulk as well as liquid. The bulk helps to move roughage through the digestive system and then to eliminate waste through the bowel.

When calories are taken as liquid and when fruit is juiced, the important bulk and fibre is lost, leaving the digestive system inactive and causing constipation or loose stools. Other health risks from excessive juice consumption include poor concentration, muscle weakness, weight gain and dental damage (from excess fruit sugars).

A typical juice fast lacks protein and essential nutrients and is simply deficient in calories for optimum physical health and energy levels. We need protein to fill us up. Unless you have adequate amounts of it, your body starts to cannibalize itself and get protein from your muscles. A juice diet contains hardly any protein so you will lose only a small amount of fat but a large amount of muscle. And if you lose muscle your metabolic rate will slow down, which exacerbates the cycle of crash dieting and subsequent weight gain.

Strict juice regimes are unsustainable in the long term, as well as unsatisfying. Juice dieters may find they have guzzled large quantities of bananas, apples and carrots, for example, but still feel hungry. This never-satiated gnawing hunger affects our mental wellbeing, mood and sleep. When you're hungry you're on edge, irritable and fatigued.

Many people adopt liquid-only diets in order to lose a lot of weight in a short space of time. Juice fasts, or fasting for prolonged periods without solid food, is really not recommended. For all the claims made for juice fasts, especially those claims around weight loss (see the opening lines of this chapter!), there is no objective scientific evidence for this. Most experts argue the opposite – that juicing and fasting encourage the kind of yo-yo cycle of craving and bingeing that is the enemy of healthy, long-term weight management. Going without solid food can be downright dangerous, causing dizziness, nausea and hypoglycaemia (low blood sugar). It's also unhealthy to get into the habit of drinking rather than eating your meals. When you cannot even enjoy a bite to eat with friends, it is socially isolating and can lead to further disordered eating behaviours and food avoidance.

Detoxing

Detoxing is another twenty-first-century obsession. Previous generations ate far less anxiously, with a varied balance of food groups and no detox neurosis. Levels of obesity, anxiety and food allergies were far lower – even though their diets were not organic, macrobiotic or biodynamic. They ate bread, potatoes, white sugar, lard and even gluten without any ill effects!

All the nutritional experts agree that the body does not need to 'detox'. Detoxification is an unscientific concept invented by the diet industry as yet another way of selling us special supplements, pills and powders. Not only does detoxing promise inner cleanliness and digestive health, it also seems to offer instant weight loss. Unsurprisingly, it has been embraced by many unqualified nutritionists, bloggers and celebrities (often endorsing their own miracle detox products). Like juicing, however, detoxing can be stressful for the body and the mind.

Detoxing is simply not necessary. Contrary to the marketing myths about hidden toxins and the need to purify, we have powerful cleaning systems inside our bodies: our liver, kidneys, bladder and bowels. They are designed to digest our food and eliminate waste products and, unless we are ill or seriously overdoing it, they carry out their function adequately. Apart from the liver, which clearly benefits from alcohol-free regeneration, the rest of our organs do not need detoxification.

At best, detoxing is a waste of time and money, at worst it can be a gateway into serious food avoidance. Healthy living is far simpler: take regular breaks from alcohol, don't smoke, eat more fruit and vegetables and less processed food. Avoid heavily polluted, traffic-choked areas and get more fresh air. And remember, you don't need to drink 20 gallons of water a day, replace solid food with fluids, restrict calories, go on juice fasts or 'flush out' toxins. Ignore the detox drivel and use your common sense.

Veganism

Vegans do not eat meat, fish, eggs, dairy or any other animal products or ingredients. Veganism is a lifestyle as well as a diet: the Vegan Society defines it as 'a way of living which seeks to exclude, as far as is possible and practicable, all forms of exploitation of, and cruelty to, animals for food, clothing or any other purpose.'

Exact estimates vary but more than half a million people in the UK are thought to have adopted a vegan diet in recent years. Almost half of all vegans are in the 15–34 age category (compared with just 14 per cent of vegans who are aged over 65) so the Vegan Society predicts that veganism will continue to grow in future as it continues to be adopted by younger generations.

There has been something of a vegan revolution online, with social-media-driven movements such as Veganuary (going vegan for the month of January) making veganism accessible and providing health information and recipes, as well as a sense of fun and community. Movements like this also help to counteract the previous sandal-wearing, muesli-munching, sanctimonious, tree-hugging, hippy stereotypes. The associations these days are now with beauty and success: from Beyoncé and Jay-Z to Joaquin Phoenix to Venus and Serena Williams, many celebrities are vocal, fashionable vegans. It's now cool to be kind to nature.

Veganism is touted as ultra-healthy and it can be – but there may be risks if the diet is deficient in nutrients or too low in calories. Specific risks include muscle wastage and insufficient cell repair, vitamin B_{12}, vitamin D and iodine deficiencies, metabolic imbalance and fatigue. Vegans risk not getting a sufficient range of protein, essential for growth, building muscle and repairing every cell in the body. Animal foods contain all the essential amino acids, but plant sources of protein can be lower. Calcium and iron can also be harder to include in sufficient amounts in a strict vegan diet.

Vitamin B_{12}, for example, regulates mood and energy levels and prevents nerve damage. It is only found in substantial quantities in animal products. This does not mean that vegetarians and vegans will necessarily be B_{12} deficient, but they may need to include fortified B_{12}-rich products such as Marmite and brewer's yeast.

Iodine is another nutrient found abundantly in animal products such as milk, eggs and white fish that may be lacking in a vegan diet. Iodine is essential for the production of thyroid hormones, which regulate the metabolism, so vegans should consider taking a supplement.

This does not mean that veganism is automatically unhealthy, but vegans (and vegetarians) do need to make a concerted effort to consume these vital nutrients in another form. Going vegan is not just a question of morality and personal ethics: it's also a question of health. These decisions matter, because our mental and physical wellbeing can be compromised by dietary deficiencies.

It is unlikely that all self-professed vegans are adhering to the strictest guidelines: many regularly drink wine and beer or still keep their favourite leather boots and handbags. And even the most committed vegan will find that avoiding all animal-derived ingredients is hard. Gelatin, whey, cysteine, casein and milk by-products and beeswax, to name but a few, are hidden in everyday foods, cosmetics and cleaning products. Many food flavourings, colourings and preservatives are derived from animal by-products. Some medications or the casing around tablets are not vegan. Many ingredients of animal, vegetable or synthetic origin are lumped together under a single name. Some products are mixed up: a vegan burger, for example, may come in a bun that contains traces of eggs or milk. Living fully vegan can be a minefield.

Interestingly, the animal welfare charity People for the Ethical Treatment of Animals (PETA) says: 'we want to emphasise that no one can avoid every single animal ingredient. Being vegan is about helping animals, not maintaining personal purity.' Strict veganism can cause health deficiencies and it can also trigger a sort of paranoia around the invisible ingredients in everyday foods, clothing, medication and household products. As a strict vegetarian I understand the impulse behind veganism – and completely support the ethical stance – but I am also aware how hard it is to avoid all animal ingredients in modern life. My own vegetarianism is driven by my concern with animal suffering and the environment, but we must also take our own mental and physical welfare into account. That PETA statement offers a balance of principle and pragmatism: if you're concerned about animal welfare this seems like a good place to start.

Clean eating

'Eating healthy, clean and nutrient-rich food fills your body with energy, nutrients and antioxidants. Imagine your cells smiling back at you saying thanks!'

'I reward my body by training hard and eating clean . . . because I'm worth it.'

'Junk food you've craved for an hour or the body you've craved for a lifetime? Your decision – #EatClean.'

'What you eat in private is eventually what you wear in public.'

'Eat clean, look lean.'

These are just a few of the many 'clean eating' motivational quotes on the online site Pinterest. Perhaps they make you laugh or roll your eyes; perhaps they make you feel anxious or angry. Clean eating is incredibly photogenic – those colourful fruit smoothies, stunning salad bowls and rainbow plates of virtuous veggies look fabulous online! Beautiful young bloggers have fuelled the 'clean eating' movement like never before. It has quickly become more than just a way of eating and is now a fully fledged aspirational lifestyle with huge commercial influence and millions of online followers.

Despite the expense, the difficult-to-source ingredients and the weird flavour combinations – do you really want beetroot in your chocolate brownies? – the clean eating movement shows no signs of slowing down. It has recently come under scrutiny, with qualified nutritional scientists highlighting the unqualified nature of its advocates and their unfounded claims. Despite being legally allowed to call themselves nutritional coaches after having taken a brief course in the subject, many of the key influencers have undertaken no academic study into dietetics or nutritional science. Their rules can be arbitrary, absolutist and are often downright unhealthy. By demonizing common ingredients such as wheat, dairy or sugar, they often end up replacing them with less healthy alternatives and adding a hefty dose of disordered eating anxiety into the mix.

The clean eating claims are sometimes so extreme that they are easy to debunk. A 'cancer-fighting cherry berry smoothie', for example, has absolutely no basis in medical fact. Although cherries are known to contain micronutrients that have been shown to have chemopreventive properties to interfere with disease, a cherry smoothie cannot do much to fight cancer. As anyone who is suffering from or has lost someone to cancer will tell you, it takes more than a smoothie to fight these painful and complex conditions.

Dr Giles Yeo, a geneticist at the University of Cambridge, examined the scientific evidence for different schools of clean eating in a BBC television *Horizon* programme and found everything from unfounded health claims and innocuous recipes to serious malpractice. Take, for example, the 'alkaline' diet, which suggests that a range of diseases are caused by eating 'acidic' foods. Or coconut oil, so beloved by clean eaters, which according to the American Heart Association has 'no known offsetting favourable effects' – and may in fact result in higher levels of low-density lipoprotein (LDL – damaging) cholesterol.

The influence of clean eating is often subtler and more persuasive, however. When we are told that we need to eliminate toxins from our body by juicing or red meat causes 'bloating, irritability, weight problems, ageing and chronic disease' or gluten causes 'a huge amount of inflammation in the gut', it's natural that we feel anxious and start to avoid everyday foods.

Quite apart from the fact that there is no scientific proof behind the clean eating 'rules' – as no foods are intrinsically clean or dirty, virtuous or sinful, good or bad – they can also have a dangerous impact on mental health. No one would argue that eating more fruit and vegetables is anything but beneficial, but in those already prone to food anxiety these principles are dangerous. Clean eating can become a gateway into disordered eating and mental illness.

Avoidance of 'processed' food, one of the main tenets of clean eating, can easily morph into a raw-food diet, for example. Eating only 'whole' foods or 'real' foods becomes increasingly restrictive. Suddenly carbohydrates like pasta are being replaced by spiralized 'courgetti', solids are being juiced or all food is avoided after 6 p.m. Vulnerable individuals or those desperate to lose weight find themselves sliding into these abnormal nutritional habits. They may become phobic about certain foods or entire food groups, putting themselves at risk of deficiencies. Essential macronutrients – carbohydrates, protein and fat – are often dangerously lacking in plant-based, raw-food or vegan diets.

Do you follow any health and wellness bloggers? Do you envy their lifestyles? Have you ever tried eating clean? Here are some experiences of others.

> ❛ *I don't count calories, grams, percentages of fat or macros. I try to only eat when I'm hungry and stop when I'm full. I don't eat any snacks, I have 2–3 meals a day and no carbs in the evening. I try to reduce my sugar intake to a minimum. I eat "clean" in the sense that I like to cook food for myself, avoid additives and consume less processed food.* ❜
> **Judith, 27**

> ❛ *I find that I'm happiest and healthiest when I don't think too much about what I eat and I don't punish myself or make food about deprivation. I definitely incorporate meals that would be classed as "clean*

eating" but I try to augment my diet with them rather than replace or substitute. I love pasta, potatoes, vegetables, meat and shellfish, and I don't want to deny myself these things . . . **)** **Letty, 29**

(I can be a sucker for "clean eating" messages. I add things that are deemed clean to my diet, such as acai, wheatgrass, spirulina, flaxseed, etc. It's very rare that I will eat white carbs – potato, bread, rice, pasta – and if I'm eating carbs it tends to be of the wholemeal variety – sweet potato, wholemeal, seeded, granary bread or spelt pasta. I guess I pretty much always police my diet. I won't allow what I deem to be unhealthy treats in the house . . . I always feel like I'm eating too much. I constantly compare how I eat to how others eat. I can eat a lot if I'm happy and enjoying something (I do love food generally) but then I feel guilt and regret. If I'm really down and depressed or super-anxious, I struggle to eat. I focus on it as a form of control and abuse myself back down to a weight I can manage or cope with . . . **)** **Karen, 30**

(I monitor what I eat very carefully. I worry significantly about my food intake to the point where food takes up 90 per cent of my daily thoughts. I'm not influenced by "clean eating" messages because a calorie is a calorie . . . I find it very difficult to enjoy food because it isn't just food any more. **)** **Niamh, 18**

(I don't count calories but I definitely watch what I eat. While I do police my diet and intake I'm still able to enjoy certain indulgences: red velvet cake, brie with a nice baguette, a crisp white wine, peanut butter! I do often get scared after indulging, though, and will fret about it for hours, even days, afterwards. When I'm around friends who are actively restricting, I definitely eat less or don't eat . . . **)** **Rachel, 28**

It's interesting how many emotions are expressed in these accounts of eating, with terms like 'guilt', 'regret' and 'anxiety' repeatedly cropping up. Feeling 'scared' after 'indulging'. One woman says, 'it isn't just food any more'. Another says she will 'abuse' herself back down to a lower weight. This highlights how close restrictive dieting can be to self-harm. When we don't respond to our hunger cues, when we restrict calories and starve to keep our bodies below their natural weight, this is a form of self-neglect, even abuse.

Orthorexia

Clean eating overlaps with, and often segues into, a more serious form of dietary restriction known as orthorexia. Orthorexia resembles anorexia and other eating disorders in the rigidity and guilt of the mindset. While those with anorexia tend to obsess about calories and weight, those with orthorexia obsess about the purity of their diet, hence the blurred boundaries with clean eating. Orthorexia is defined as a 'fixation with righteous or correct eating' – but what begins as a healthy attempt to improve one's lifestyle can morph into an unhealthy fixation with the 'perfect' diet.

As in clean eating, orthorexia thrives in a society obsessed with 'wellness' in which we are urged to lose weight, count calories, avoid artificial additives and preservatives, and beware hidden toxins. Individuals with severe orthorexia may find their social interactions limited by their need for 'pure' and natural food. Relationships and family life may be hindered by intrusive obsessions regarding healthy eating, and sleeping patterns suffer, as does concentration, work and daily functioning.

As with clean eating, the orthorexic mindset is to become preoccupied with unscientific notions of toxins and chemicals. It focuses on purity and the need to cleanse and detoxify the body from inside. Even the occasional 'bad' food, sweet treat or processed substance will induce guilt, which makes socializing difficult. It can lead to self-loathing, low self-esteem and isolation. On top of the rigid eating rules, many people with orthorexia are also addicted to intense exercise, which adds up to a lifestyle of anxiety, self-denial and restriction.

Food and our lifestyles

If food were simply fuel for our bodies, we could just swallow a daily 2,000-calorie pill and be done with it. Most people wouldn't choose that, however, even if such a joyless, Orwellian food-pill were available. We gaze into patisserie windows or linger as we pass the bakery, we dream about food and look forward to eating. Mealtimes punctuate our days: breakfast gets us going first thing, lunchtime gives us a reason to glance away from the computer screen, dinner is a way to unwind in the evenings. Food is at the heart of what it means to be human, to share and shop and socialize with others, to meet up with friends, to travel to new countries and explore new cultures.

A healthy, balanced diet also improves our mood and emotional wellbeing. Levels of the feel-good brain chemical serotonin are dependent on the food we consume, which explains the low mood that often results from low-carbohydrate diets. And diets are miserable because most of us don't like restricting what we eat. Humans are not designed to be hungry: hunger makes us uncomfortable, restless, on edge. From an evolutionary perspective we are driven to seek out calories in order to stay warm, to procreate, to be stronger than the next tribe in the next village. The survival instinct is strong.

Most diets not only police how much we eat but also what we eat. So it's a double-whammy of calorie restriction and deprivation, being banned from eating the things we love. The substances that diets tend to target – fat, carbohydrates, sugar – are also the substances we crave.

Deprivation of any kind feels bad. Not being allowed to eat what you love makes you sad. And not only does it leave us empty, it also leaves us isolated. When you cannot freely enjoy your food, you cannot really enjoy the company of others. Where's the fun in going to a restaurant with friends when they're ordering glorious plates of food and bottles of wine, and you're having a salad and a glass of fizzy water? Where's the enjoyment in cooking with the person you love when you can't share the same experience? Where's the indulgence of a birthday or Christmas celebration when you're miserably carb-free, fat-free, dairy-free or all three? As well as being our fuel, food is also pleasure and flavour, indulgence and ritual, culture and identity, home and love.

Not only do diets make us miserable but also they don't work. The entire diet industry is predicated on repeat custom: people coming back again and again to try and lose the same weight. If diets worked, we would only have to do them once. In fact, an estimated 90 per cent of people who lose weight by dieting will regain it within two years. Diets are not only a multi-billion dollar industry, but also something of an occupational obsession: in the past ten years it is estimated that around 70 per cent of the adult female population and 30 per cent of adult men have been on a diet. (Hence the joke that there are two types of women: those who are watching their weight and those who pretend not to be.)

The endless cycle of restriction sets up an unhealthy yo-yo effect, whereby the body gains and loses the same 5 or 10 kilos. Repeated weight gain and loss puts the body under excessive stress, as well as causing depression and a sense of failure and despair. People go from diet to diet, hoping to find the miracle formula, but of course it doesn't exist. And since the body does not want to starve, it responds to restrictive diets by slowing your metabolism, which makes it harder to lose weight, leading to a cycle of overeating, bingeing and yo-yo dieting.

How do diets mess up your metabolism? Instead of consuming calories, burning these calories as fuel and then needing more, the body hangs on to weight, usually fat, as a safeguard against the dietary deprivation to come and slows its metabolism down. The more we diet, the more we confuse our metabolism and mess up our body's natural 'set point'.

Set point

The set point in our body is the level at which a variable physiological state, such as body temperature or weight, tends to stabilize. The set point theory suggests that our body systems are automatically regulated to remain within a certain range, like an inner thermostat for body weight. The set point is the level at which the body functions optimally.

Set point theory argues that the body will fight to remain at or around its natural set point, in weight terms usually a range of 5–10 kilos, within which you will be comfortable and function well. Just as we have different eye and hair colours, so we all have a different set point. This is determined by our individual biology and genetics, not by diet or exercise. This theory explains why some people are naturally thinner or fatter than others and why some people are able to eat a lot without gaining weight, whereas others gain weight easily and struggle to lose weight and keep it off.

Set point theory is enlightening to anyone with an eating disorder or anyone who is constantly battling their own appetite to try to lose weight. Learning to accept the fact that your body needs to be at a certain weight is a good way to stop the vicious cycle of dieting and disordered eating. Drastically restricting your food intake simply slows down your metabolism, as your body tries to adjust to fewer calories. The more you try to go below your natural set point range, the harder your body will strive to retain its natural weight. Accepting the set point theory is an important aspect of mental and physical wellbeing: instead of endlessly struggling against our bodies, we can start to accept them.

Disordered eating

Is my claim that clean eating can be a gateway into mental illness a little far-fetched? I don't think so. I have spoken to hundreds of women whose healthy diet morphed into strict, pure, clean eating, which morphed into orthorexia or even anorexia. The worlds of everyday dieting and life-threatening eating disorders are both closer and further apart than we realize. Of course, most people can go on a diet and lose a few kilos, then look forward to enjoying their favourite foods again. But others cannot. And if you are vulnerable to an eating disorder, restricting food can be fatal.

Dieting is the most important single predictor of developing an eating disorder. In 2016, the American Academy of Pediatrics issued new guidelines on preventing eating disorders and obesity. Their key recommendation was that parents should never talk to their children about diets or weight. According to the report, 40 per cent of those admitted to hospital or clinics for eating disorders are dieters who have got out of control, tipping into anorexia or bulimia.

We live in a society obsessed with dieting, weight loss and body image. We see thousands of images every day on our smartphones and tablets or in magazines, and scrolling, filtering and airbrushing our own photos has become second nature, all trying to present the best possible version of ourselves on social media. In a strange contradiction, we are also obsessed with food and bombarded with mouth-watering images of the newest craze, the latest superfood, juice cleanse or protein supplement. Weight loss used to be primarily a female concern, and primarily an adolescent concern, but extreme anxiety around body shape and weight is now affecting men and even young children.

Sadly, social media is a gift to eating disorders, offering unrealistic images of the perfect body, food and fitness lifestyle. It fuels the highly damaging compare-and-despair syndrome and exacerbates feelings of insecurity and worthlessness, particularly among the most anxious and vulnerable young people. They feel they should be working out harder for longer and eating less; they should look like the YouTube vloggers, models or foodies they idolize online. But the realities of anorexia, bulimia and binge eating are far from glamorous: no one Instagrams their teeth rotting from excess stomach acid or their fingers calloused from repeatedly vomiting.

Under pressure from social media and the widespread culture of dieting, perfectionism and body anxiety, many young women respond by bingeing, purging and self-harming. Sadly, adolescence is an especially dangerous time for undereating because the body is still developing: it ideally requires around 2,500 high-quality calories a day. Many teenage girls at this age try to limit themselves to fewer than 1,000 calories a day, cutting out the calcium, fats and other essential nutrients their growing body needs. And the more weight they lose, the more social approval they receive.

So, although eating disorders are more complex than normal diets, they do begin as diets. Although the majority of dieters will not become dangerously anorexic or bulimic, a significant proportion will. The prevalence of diet-talk in every workplace and school, on every TV show, magazine or website, sends out a clear message: thinner is better. Unsurprisingly, this inculcates the diet mindset among young people and adults and may lead to a lifetime of always trying to lose weight, of restricting calories, vomiting after meals or binge eating in secret.

The binge–starve cycle

When we stop responding to our natural hunger cues, starving ourselves when we should be eating, the body becomes confused. It ends up feeling hungry all the time. Individuals experience a bottomless, ravenous hunger that no amount of food can satisfy. Binge eating is out-of-control eating, consuming calories out of all proportion to what the body actually wants or needs. As one woman emailed me, 'During binges the eating is uncontrollable, like an out-of-body experience, just cramming food in. These insane cravings for fat and sugar and carbs, I literally cannot stop.'

Her honesty highlights not only the uncontrollable nature of bingeing, but also the fixation and uncontrollable craving for fats, sugar and carbohydrates, all the foods that are demonized on diets. She 'confessed' that, at her worst, a binge episode could contain as many as 10,000–20,000 calories (well over a week's worth of calories within a normal eating pattern). The sadness in her email was palpable – I wanted to reach out and reassure her that she wasn't the only one struggling with over- or undereating – but I understood her shame. Bingeing is dangerous for the body and distressing for the mind, often leaving the individual with an overwhelming sense of self-disgust.

Variety is the spice of life

The stricter your diet, the narrower the range of food you will be permitted and the greater your risk of nutritional deficiencies. Dietary restriction is an unhealthy habit, not to say monotonous. To be genuinely healthy we need to consume as wide a range of micronutrients as possible: these are the essential vitamins and minerals that power everything in our body. The most important micronutrients include calcium, iron, potassium, magnesium, zinc, vitamins D and C and the B vitamins, and these are required for everything from blood clotting and nerve functioning to cell repair and muscle contraction. They are also necessary for mood regulation and the nervous system, immune health, wound healing and strong teeth and bones.

The best way to ensure your supply of these vital micronutrients is to eat many different foods from day to day. When we talk about eating the colours of the rainbow, it is this variety we should be aiming for: reds and yellows, oranges and greens, purples and so on. These deep colours indicate rich phytonutrients, biologically active substances that protect plants from viruses and bacteria and help protect humans from disease. Brightness, especially for fruit and vegetables, is a reliable indicator: think peppers, strawberries, spinach, aubergines, blueberries. Visualize a market stall displaying the most colourful fruit and veg and include as many as you can, within season. These are bursting with vitamins and minerals that can be powerful anti-inflammatories, improve blood flow and boost immunity.

Be curious and open to new food experiences. You do not have to be a skilled cook to be adventurous: it could be as simple as buying a different kind of pasta, trying a new fish or meat, Quorn or tofu or experimenting with unfamiliar herbs and spices in your cooking. You could sample your friend's dish at a restaurant or recreate your favourite meal from a holiday, keeping your taste buds on their toes.

Strict dietary rules are bad for your physical health but also damaging to your mental wellbeing. As we have seen, labelling foods as sinful, processed or impure or eliminating entire food groups is a dangerous path to go down. It puts you at risk of developing restrictive and neurotic eating habits. You may become preoccupied with the 'perfect' diet and unable to eat with others. What starts as health-consciousness can easily become health-obsessiveness and may slip into an actual eating disorder. Constantly suppressing your appetite is hell. Deprivation is bad for your body and bad for your mind.

Moderation: the Holy Grail

The ancient Greek 'father of medicine' Hippocrates said, 'If we could give every individual the right amount of nourishment and exercise, not too little and not too much, we would have found the safest way to health.' Hippocrates nails it – balance is the safest way to health.

The answer, of course, is to enjoy all things in moderation, but that is harder than it sounds. In fact, for most of us it's impossible. Obviously, we all know what we should be doing: balancing calories in against calories out, eating fresh, wholesome food and being physically active every day. However hard it is, we should strive for balance. Cutting out specific foods or, more often, entire food groups, is not conducive to either a healthy body or a healthy mind. Exercise addiction is also unhealthy and potentially dangerous. Extreme restriction, bingeing, starving and exercising excessively are risky behaviours and will also make your life a misery.

Allowing ourselves to enjoy a plentiful diet, balanced in protein, carbohydrates and good fats, rich in vitamins and minerals – and yes, a small amount of 'sinful' food – this has to be the Holy Grail. Moderation, rather than miracle diets, is the healthiest mindset.

80:20 principle

Remember, food doesn't need to be super-healthy or virtuous all the time! The 80:20 rule is a reasonable guide to follow, whereby you eat nutritious food 80 per cent of the time and allow yourself to indulge in treats for 20 per cent of the time. It's hardly scientific, but it makes sense – and it works within normal life. You don't need to deprive yourself of pizza, Chinese takeaway or the night out with cocktails, you can still have the chocolate if you're craving it, because you are not eating like that all of the time. The 80:20 principle is a really useful framework, especially for anyone who has had disordered eating in the past, as it encourages you to fill up on nutritious whole foods, but not to deprive yourself or ban 'naughty' foods.

I follow the 80:20 philosophy, very loosely, in my head – and the vagueness is sort of the point! This isn't about strict rules or counting macronutrients, but simply a rough tally so that your calories are mostly 'healthy' but you have the leeway to enjoy tasty goodies too. If a wedding or party is coming up, you can indulge in delicious celebratory food without guilt.

It is an approach based on balance and, crucially, it is relaxed enough not to encourage restriction and anxiety to creep back in. Life becomes miserable when you can't eat what you love and many of us have learned that our hearts need cake as well as kale! I recently bought some onion bread for the first time, on a whim – a warm, freshly baked loaf studded with melty cheese and caramelized onion – and it was utterly delicious. Eating that did more good for my soul than any amount of celery.

Your food, your choice

Above all, it is essential to eat food that makes you feel good. It's no good following regimes that are touted as healthy but make you feel awful. We all have different taste buds and metabolic systems and guts. Get to know your own digestive system.

Have the confidence to decide what your body needs. If certain foods leave you feeling bloated or sleepy or instantly hungry again, they are probably not right for you. If carbohydrates give you energy, enjoy them; if protein makes you feel strong, go for it. Don't cut out caffeine if that morning espresso is one of your daily pleasures; don't eliminate dairy if you really love cheese. Life is for living, after all.

The best strategy for physical and mental wellbeing is to make the choice to end the anxiety and just to eat what works for you, within reason: food that makes your body feel nourished, doesn't make you gain or lose too much weight; food you can afford, doesn't wreck the environment and tastes good.

Many of these choices simply are not available to the rest of the world: globally, around 1 billion people are classed as undernourished, around 2 billion are classed as overnourished and another 2 billion live in what's known as 'hidden hunger', on a diet of low quality and lacking in essential micronutrients. Eating in affluent developed countries can be a minefield of complexity and anxiety, but we should remember the millions who live without food choices. We should try to value the freedom we have. If we can break away from the cycle of excess and denial, we can appreciate the privilege of plentiful, nutritious food. If we can rid our vocabulary of virtue and vice, good foods and bad, if we can ignore the modern obsession with weight loss and learn to trust our own appetites, only then can we re-establish a happy, healthy relationship with food.

Eating well contributes immeasurably to our mental and physical wellbeing. Food is fuel and it's also pleasure. Guilt and anxiety have no place on your plate.

Exercise, healthy body and wellbeing

> If you are in a bad mood go for a walk. If you are still in a bad mood
> go for another walk.   Hippocrates

Exercise is essential for wellbeing on so many levels, starting with the simplest: it's what the human body is designed to do. Think of our pre-historic ancestors in constant movement, walking, running, jumping, lifting, chasing and hunting in order to fend off predators, to build shelter, fetch water and find food. Life was an ongoing struggle to ensure their own survival. Even in more recent centuries, even for our grand-parents, shopping, washing, baking and cleaning was an endless process of hard physical labour. For many people in the world, living without access to running water or online supermarket deliveries, gruelling physical activity is still an everyday necessity.

It's not only our bodies that need to move. The Royal College of Psychiatrists reports that 'for mild depression, physical activity can be as good as antidepressants or psychological treatments like cognitive behavioural therapy'. There are many reasons why exercise is good for our heads.

- Physical activity activates certain brain chemicals associated with mood, particularly dopamine and serotonin, which the brain cells use to communicate with each other. Exercise also enhances your cognitive functioning, making you sharper and more alert.
- Exercise stimulates the release of chemicals called endorphins. These interact with brain receptors to reduce the perception of pain – acting

as a sort of natural painkiller – and are sometimes considered to be as potent as morphine. Endorphins, also produced by massage, acupuncture and deep breathing, are known as 'feel-good' chemicals.

- Exercise seems to reduce harmful changes in the brain caused by stress.
- Exercise helps you escape from stressors at work, at home and in your environment – it literally gives you headspace.
- Exercise helps you sleep. It gives you energy. And it boosts your body confidence and your self-esteem.
- Exercising outdoors in nature has profound soothing and restorative qualities.
- Exercise gives you a sense of control over your life. It helps you feel capable, healthy and strong. It's also very uplifting.

We are hard-wired for movement and that is why exercise makes us feel good. Motion and exertion take us back to our primal roots and remind us that we are human beings, not cyborgs or avatars or social media brands.

As mentioned, exercise benefits your brain, because it gets the blood pumping and improves oxygen flow to all the organs – including the little grey cells in our head. This increased blood flow allows nutrients to be carried to the brain and more toxins and waste products to be efficiently disposed of. This in turn enhances cognitive functioning, including concentration, focus and memory.

Exercise also helps the adrenal system to work more effectively, helping you cope with stress and daily challenges. In circular fashion the brain relies on the adrenal system to produce healthy levels of the hormones it needs to function properly.

Being physically active is one of the best things you can do for your overall wellbeing. Whether you schedule in formal exercise – a regular gym workout or yoga class – or you just build it into your daily routine, the benefits for your mind and body are wide-ranging and immediate. You will see and feel the benefits from day one: every walk, run or swim, every ten minutes spent skipping in the back garden, will give you an instant boost. Not only does it improve blood and oxygen flow around the body, thus strengthening your muscles, lungs and cardiovascular system, but it also gets the endorphins flowing, which lifts your mood.

The benefits of physical activity are also cumulative, so you will notice your wellbeing improving the more you can commit to a regular daily practice. Again, this can be completely informal: ten minutes stretching while the dinner cooks, say, or a walk with the dog. Seeing this steady progress in your mood and fitness is hugely motivating and will inspire you to keep going. Here are just a few of the reasons to get moving.

No time, no money?

Gym membership isn't cheap – and the posher yoga and pilates classes can be eye-wateringly expensive! – but the great outdoors is yours for free. Truly, being physically active needn't cost you a penny. No matter where you live, in the inner city or the wildest countryside, no one can charge you for going for a walk, a bike ride or a run.

Being active also needn't be time-consuming. When surveyed, over half of UK adults say they 'don't have time' for regular exercise, but is this really the case? While we lead busy lives, working, studying, commuting, parenting, we also spend plenty of time watching Netflix, browsing online or glued to our screens, physically immobile. It's not all wasted time, but it's certainly not active! The increasingly sedentary nature of our lives is a health risk and exercise is a fantastic corrective to those hours we spend hunched over our phones and tablets.

Good for girls

Sport is particularly powerful for the fairer sex, in terms of balancing hormonal fluctuations and improving self-esteem. Sadly, girls and women do not always take part. Whether it is concerns over looking sweaty and unattractive or simply that gyms and football pitches are seen as places for men, female participation in sport is consistently lower than male. Figures released by the Office for National Statistics in 2018 revealed that, in the UK, boys aged between 8 and 15 spend almost twice as much time on sports activities as girls of the same age – although when they did participate, both girls and boys reported similar levels of satisfaction and enjoyment.

The biggest drop-off in girls participating in sports activities occurs during the transition from primary to secondary school and this is attributed to declining body confidence during adolescence. The Youth Sports Trust has said that 'Lack of activity correlates to a greater decline in wellbeing among children and teenagers. All the evidence suggests that if you're inactive you're likely to be less happy.' This is backed up by other recent research into young women's mental health (by University College London) showing that 1 in 4 teenage girls suffer from depression, compared with just 9 per cent of boys the same age.

Healthy habits start early and regular physical activity can be both empowering and enjoyable. It strengthens us in both mind and body. Young or old, as women we should make time to get active, to get out of breath, to get gloriously sweaty – and to feel the joy of movement.

Green therapy

The evidence is overwhelming: being in the great outdoors has such positive effects on your mental health, and exercising outside has proven benefits for your mind as well as your body. Numerous research studies have shown that exercising outdoors reduces levels of cortisol, the hormone released when you are under pressure.

Being outdoors – even without being active – is proven to be good for our minds, bodies and souls. In 1984, the researcher Roger Ulrich found that hospital patients appeared to recover more quickly from surgery in rooms with green views. Further scientific evidence backs up the health benefits of being in or near greenery.

- A view of nature helps the body to heal faster than having no view when we're unwell.
- A view of nature can also help us to regain our focus when we're distracted.
- When we're stressed, images of a natural landscape can slow our heart rates, relax our muscles and promote a feeling of calm.
- Natural daylight is a vital source of vitamin D and regulates the production of essential hormones such as melatonin and serotonin, needed for healthy brains and sleep.
- Exposure to natural daylight also keeps us alert and is a great mood booster.

Mental health walking and running clubs are springing up all over the UK, dedicated to improving not only physical fitness but also mental fitness. The concept is about sharing thoughts and emotions while exercising and it can be a powerful tool in recovery. Walking and talking is a good way to share personal problems without the pressure of a one-to-one clinical or consulting room environment. Many of us find that anxiety is reduced and our thoughts flow differently when we are outside and active. As a writer I know that going for a walk can help unblock writing problems and the same is true of other emotional blockages in our lives. Simple physical movement helps us to gain a fresh mental perspective.

Walking also has the added benefit of being environmentally friendly, free of charge and faff-free – no preparation, special equipment or gym gear required! Walking is often faster than public transport and it is certainly more reliable. When you compare it to crowded commuter trains, long bus queues or stuffy journeys underground, walking is a win–win option. It's a clean, green workout that costs nothing and gets you exactly where you need to go. So if you live in a town or city, could you walk some or all of the way to work?

Outside or in?

As we have seen, several studies have compared the benefits of outdoors versus indoor exercise, showing that fresh air, greenery and even just views of nature are beneficial to mental health and physical recovery. What about from a sports performance point of view: should we work out outdoors or inside; does it make any difference to energy levels, capacity and results?

Conclusions vary, but the basic message is the same: as long as you're using your muscles and raising your heart rate, you're on the right track. The research into running, however, is interesting. Findings consistently indicate that running outdoors, for example, rather than on a static treadmill indoors, enhances the overall experience and increases wellbeing. Here are some of the reasons why.

Running outdoors increases satisfaction and results. A Duke University study from 2004 found that treadmill runners ran more slowly, reported higher rated perceived exertion and experienced less satisfaction than runners running outside. So indoor running feels harder, delivers fewer benefits and is less enjoyable than outdoor running.

Running outdoors challenges your biomechanics. When you are running outside, you are adjusting subconsciously to every slope, stone, incline or mound of grass, weaving around pedestrians, crossing roads, leaping over puddles and so on. You are in constant movement and this is great for the muscles and ligaments in the feet, for biomechanics and for overall balance and flexibility.

Running outdoors is also less repetitive. Treadmill running may cause repetitive strain injuries, such as shin splints, because the foot is falling continuously in the same way, in the same place. In outdoor terrain – whether on city streets or grassy trails – the load and cushioning of the feet are constantly varied. Other changes in gait and stride have been observed in habitual treadmill runners that do not happen when you are running in a more natural environment, where your body can adapt to different gradients, acceleration and other variables.

Running may not be your thing – and that's totally fine. Some people find it deeply therapeutic, others find it mind-numbingly boring. It tends to be rather solitary, which is right for some of us but not others. You may be more of a swimmer, you may prefer lifting weights, doing online classes in your own home, taking the dog for a walk or just strolling to the supermarket.

Collective exercise is also great for your wellbeing. As well as those mental health groups mentioned earlier, group classes or team sports are fantastic for boosting your mood and connecting with others. Exercising with a friend provides additional motivation, because it's much harder to pull out if you've arranged to run or work out with someone else. The same goes for team sports, because you can't let the team down!

On your bike

Cycling is another functional form of exercise that gets you exactly where you need to go. It's minimum fuss and maximum efficiency, with the bonus of being green, clean and virtually free (give or take the odd puncture and bike service!).

Cycling has remarkable health benefits, as a study from the University of Birmingham and King's College London in 2018 revealed. Scientists conducted tests on 125 amateur cyclists between the ages of 55 and 79 and compared them with healthy adults who did not exercise regularly. They found that the cyclists preserved muscle mass and strength with age while maintaining stable levels of body fat and cholesterol. Even more significantly, they found that the anti-ageing effects appeared to extend to the immune system, with cycling actually holding back the process of ageing and rejuvenating the body's natural defences and immunity. Regular cyclists of this age group were generating as many T-cells (a type of immune cell) as young people were.

Although this research focused on older cyclists, the health benefits are applicable to all ages and countless other studies have reported similarly positive effects. A 2017 study in the *British Medical Journal* found that cycling cut the risk of death from all causes by more than 40 per cent and cut the risk of cancer and heart disease by 45 per cent. The pedal-power is not only physical: researchers have also found that cycling improves your mental health and that those who commute by bike are less prone to depression.

Cycling can be as committed or casual as you like, in everything from the model of bike you choose to the gear you wear. Some people join cycling clubs and race around the country in head-to-toe Lycra, while the rest of us happily pedal around town in our jeans or even party clothes. Some days I'm challenging the bike couriers at breakneck speed, others I'm freewheeling along just enjoying the views. As long as you are aware of the traffic and wear a helmet, you can take cycling entirely at your own pace.

Cycling is also low impact, which makes it the ideal option for those who may have overdone exercise in the past (see below). A good bike ride releases those feel-good endorphins, boosts your mood and energizes you, without exerting undue stress on weakened or fragile bones.

Cycling also improves our collective wellbeing: the more people take to two wheels, the fewer the individual journeys in cars and taxis and the lower the levels of traffic congestion and pollution. Towns across the UK are following the lead of the great European cycling cities such as Amsterdam, with more than 2 million Brits now cycling at least once a week according to British Cycling UK. And governments have responded quickly to the urban cycling movement, providing more dedicated bike lanes and so-called 'Superhighways', bike-locking spaces and public bike-hire schemes for those who do not own their own, as well as Cycle to Work tax-free incentives.

London has seen a genuine revolution in the people's pedal-power over the past few years – I regularly see roads in the City of London thronged with cyclists during the morning rush hour (to the displeasure of many motorists!). In Zone 1 during the morning commute, it is estimated that 32 per cent of all vehicles on the roads are now bicycles.

On some main roads, the figure is as high as 70 per cent. This is an inspiring example of how individuals contribute to the wellbeing of our society, improving air quality and reducing exhaust fumes and pollution. Cycling makes our cities safer, cleaner and greener and keeps them moving.

Strong women

Cardio activity like cycling and running is excellent for the cardiovascular system, raising the heart rate, increasing blood and oxygen flow throughout the body, boosting physical resilience and endurance, balancing hormones and even slowing down the cell ageing process. It is also important to build and maintain muscle mass, however, and this is where weight training comes in.

Many of us, especially women, focus on cardio for its obvious calorie-burning and fat-loss benefits. We fixate on losing weight, shedding fat, getting smaller and lighter, and neglect our muscles and bones, the vital inner scaffolding that holds us together. Then there are the negative stereotypes: female weight training has unattractive connotations, conjuring up images of bulging body-builders in bikinis. The weights section of the average gym is still a predominantly male domain, with highly muscled men sweating and grunting around the squat racks.

And strength training will make us bulk up and gain weight, right? Wrong. Compared with men, women have much lower potential for building muscle due to much lower levels of the key muscle-building hormone testosterone. Due to our hormonal profile, it is very unlikely that any woman will bulk up or become excessively muscular without radically increasing calorie intake and introducing body-building supplements or anabolic steroids. In fact, regular strength training is one of the most effective ways to burn fat, build muscle and maintain a healthy, lean physique.

Strength training also boosts your metabolism by speeding up your resting metabolic rate. This is because it takes your body more calories to maintain muscle than it does to maintain fat. Strength training also increases bone density, builds a stronger heart, reduces blood pressure and improves blood flow, halts muscle loss, controls blood sugar, improves cholesterol levels and helps your balance and coordination.

We all lose muscle mass as we age, and it is particularly important for women (with the risk of osteoporosis or brittle bones) to maintain a strong musculoskeletal system as we get older. So, despite being seen as a traditionally male activity, weightlifting has genuine benefits for women.

If you're not a fan of gyms, there are plenty of opportunities to incorporate strength training into your everyday life. This could be informal, such as lugging around heavy shopping, children or bottles of water! Or you could buy some equipment to use at home, such as kettlebells, dumbbells, resistance bands and skipping ropes. Medicine balls or stability balls are great for strengthening your core and a basic yoga mat will keep you comfortable as you work out.

Strength training is also fantastic for your self-image and mental health: research shows that women who train regularly are more positive about their bodies and less preoccupied with losing weight. This makes sense: why should we want to shrink ourselves? Increasing our physical presence in the world, rather than diminishing it, is empowering. Becoming stronger gives us a better chance of coping with physical and mental adversity. It gives us resilience to stand up to illness or depression, and it protects against the inevitable muscular decline of ageing. It teaches us persistence and bravery, and makes us proud of our power instead of ashamed of our shape. It boosts our positivity and improves our self-image. Becoming stronger also makes us safer out and about in the big bad world. So forget the negative stereotypes and get lifting. A stronger body is a fitter, leaner, happier body.

Going too far . . .

The health benefits of exercise are undeniable, but it can go wrong. You should be able to start and you should be able to stop. For a minority – and I include myself in this – it becomes an unhealthy compulsion and that's where things get complicated.

Like healthy eating, exercise is promoted as an unalloyed good, something we should all be aiming for. It's hard to avoid the constant reminders that we should all be on diets (wrong) and we should all be at the gym (wrong). Exercise is a healthy discipline, but it shouldn't make you ill. There is a fine line between positive willpower and damaging self-punishment.

For anyone who has become unhealthily obsessed or addicted to exercise, willpower is a dangerous thing. Willpower fuels the self-punishing mindset, driving you to do more more more on less less less, criticizing you, goading you, taunting you inside your own head and in the mirror. The exercise addiction bullies you into driving yourself harder, further, faster, never allowing you to feel good enough, never allowing you to rest. In the depths of anorexia I was in the grip of this kind of exercise addiction – and utterly out of control. The addiction, not me, was in control.

Most individuals have a healthy measure of willpower that allows them to exercise safely. It takes willpower to push yourself out of the house for a run on a cold dark morning, but you probably know you'll feel great for it afterwards. If you're exercising safely, there will be days where you can't be bothered, when you wake up and think 'forget it', switch off the alarm, skip the run and stay in bed – and that's healthy. You should be able to listen to your body when it's tired or not in the mood, because recovery from exercise is as important as exercise itself. Taking days off is important both mentally and physically: even elite athletes have rest days to repair their muscles and refresh their minds.

For some, what starts as a healthy habit can transform into an unhealthy addiction. In the depths of my addiction, exercise was no longer a choice but a compulsion. I wasn't choosing to go on those endless, punishing morning runs, so much as being bullied into it by the voice inside my head. The exercise addiction fuelled the anorexia and vice versa: the more I ran the less I ate and the more miserable I became. If

I didn't exercise every day, I was plagued with guilt and anxiety. I was physically running myself into the ground.

The following women share their experiences of exercise and how they are trying to find a healthy balance.

❝ *I take a valuable daily walk, this provides time for me to think and ground myself, get fresh air and generally makes me feel better. I get anxious if I don't have a walk as it's part of my routine. Previously I became obsessive about exercise – particularly running – so now I avoid this. I've learned the warning signs and have to monitor myself carefully.* ❞ **Rachel, 28**

❝ *I'm a huge fan of running and I rely heavily on the endorphins it gives me. I feel better for doing it, because it increases my energy all round. Then again, I often feel guilty or fat for not doing it. Running allows me some time out to literally pound the pavements. I feel saner, clearer in my thoughts and more composed when I can "run it out".* ❞ **Karen, 30**

❝ *Exercise has never been something I've done, and I feel horrendous for it. I'm disgusted at how little exercise I do.* ❞ **Gemma, 21**

❝ *I enjoy exercising but I try not to put pressure on myself or set too many goals. I'm not a passionate walker but I'll happily hike for a few days on holiday. I've recently found an outdoors exercise class I enjoy, and I like team activities and things that aren't solitary.* ❞ **Letty, 29**

❝ *Having previously had issues with over-exercising, I know this is an area I have to monitor closely. In a society obsessed with gym culture, this is pretty tough. I have to constantly remind myself that my health needs are different from society's health needs – my body does not need to be pummelled on the cross-trainer, quite the opposite. Even so, this is something anorexia hates and continually taunts me for. I try to "limit" my exercise to walking – let's be honest, countryside dog walks are far better than stuffy gyms!* ❞ **Yasmin, 24**

❝ *I used to be a professional runner, so exercise has always been a massive part of my life. I retired from athletics a couple of years ago and work 9 to 5, so I don't exercise anywhere near as much as I used to – although I still exercise a lot. The times when I don't go I feel guilty about it – but I find that if I talk through with someone why I haven't gone and get their "approval" I feel better. My current exercise regime is Monday to Friday and then I have weekends off. I see my boyfriend at weekends so that's our time together. I try and go for sociable exercise now, it's so much easier to get out of the door when you have people to meet. And it's more enjoyable.* ❞ **Emma, 29**

These women struggle with feelings of guilt when they do not exercise but have mostly managed to stay in control. By acknowledging their own tendency to over-exercise, and by monitoring themselves carefully, they avoid falling back into the cycle of anxiety and self-punishment. Their strategies for staying well include taking weekends off, for example, going for gentle walks or exercising with friends.

For others, their compulsion is linked with weight and body anxiety and disordered eating and still clearly causes intense mental anguish.

❝ *I'm not allowed to exercise much any more because of my anorexia but I used to exercise compulsively after everything I ate. I'd say exercise did me more harm than good – but I can see it can be great for healthy people and it's good for mental health. I do still feel guilty for not doing as much exercise now but I don't have the energy . . . there comes a point when you just have to listen to the professionals.* ❞ **Ellie, 17**

❝ *I walk to and from university each day. I walk into town and to the supermarket. Public transport is there but I feel guilty for using it. If I don't have my daily walk to and from university, then I make up for it by walking somewhere else and / or not eating or else I won't feel good. I don't use the gym any more because I get obsessed.* ❞ **Niamh, 18**

     ❝ I really need to get back into exercise for my physical and mental health. However, I used to suffer from bulimia, so trying to find a balance between doing exercise out of enjoyment and self-discipline is something I struggle with. ❞ **Taylor, 19**

     ❝ I was addicted to exercise throughout my eating disorder; now I have become fearful of overdoing it and it becoming an addiction again. Exercise was a form of self-punishment so I never got any joy out of it. ❞ **Sophie, 19**

I find that last comment very sad. Exercise – which, after all, is just a grown-up form of play – should never bring us that low.

So how much is too much, and how does healthy activity make us ill? It is impossible to generalize because we all have different physiologies and different mental health histories. It is probably fine for someone robust who is consuming a high-calorie diet with plenty of carbohydrates and fat to do intense, regular workouts. On the other hand, someone with a history of disordered eating should definitely not be working out: for these individuals excessive exercise can exert a dangerous toll on an already malnourished body.

It is often assumed that the less you eat, the less exercise you can do, but in anorexia, although the duration and intensity of exercise increases, calorie intake does not. Many people persevere with strenuous physical exertion to the point of near-collapse. Excessive exercise makes the individual lose yet more weight and places the weakened heart under stress. It damages osteoporotic or fragile bones and broken bones and fractures are common in individuals with anorexia. It also causes muscle wasting: when there is no fat to burn as fuel the body begins to eat away at its own muscle. All these problems are exacerbated by an insufficient intake of protein to rebuild muscles, and calcium and vitamins for healthy bones.

The positives and negatives of exercise can get horribly mixed – we start doing something healthy and get locked into a cycle of exhausting self-harming behaviour. This woman relates her own struggles and how she is gradually finding her way to a healthier place.

❝ *I think it's good to exercise regularly, but I'm aware I often overdo it. When I hit a big blow, stress, anxiety or depression, all I want to do is stop eating and run. I used to exercise twice a day every weekday, up at 5.30 a.m. for the gym before work and then I would run the 5 miles home. I cut down a lot a few years ago but sometimes when I think of it I feel guilty and like I was happier then – I was tiny and constantly fuelled by endorphins. It's incredibly difficult to stop completely – for me it's a work in progress.* ❞ **Karen, 30**

However you exercise, it should be a positive choice and it should be enjoyable. Exercise should not become a compulsion. You should be able to choose when you exercise and for how long. You shouldn't push yourself to exercise through exhaustion or injury. When it's making you miserable and anxious, warning bells should go off. Ignore the messages from society and the media: whatever you hear about exercising five times a week, burning fat or shedding kilos or getting those rock-hard abs, you are an individual. If you're struggling with mental or physical illness, your body may not be strong enough for exercise. Only you can know what's going on inside your head and it's essential to listen to it.

If any of these women's experiences resonate with you, you may be in a difficult or addictive relationship with exercise. Don't despair. Recovery from exercise addiction is possible and definitely worth aiming for. You may need to go 'cold turkey' for a while – I had to give up running completely while in recovery from anorexia – but you should eventually be able to introduce exercise back into your life. Gentle activity, as opposed to gruelling self-punishment, can be a positive part of mental and physical rehabilitation.

Salute the sun . . .

If you're overdoing it, if you're frail or underweight or you're simply aware that exercise has become an unhealthy compulsion, yoga is an ideal alternative. Yoga and meditation help hugely with stress, anxiety and depression and have many other health benefits too. Whether you practise it for physical fitness, to help with aches and pains, to stay supple, to counteract stress or anxiety, to cope with tough times, to get headspace in a busy schedule, to challenge yourself or simply for pure enjoyment, yoga is a healthy habit. Recent research by American and Dutch scientists found that it is as effective at combating heart disease as traditional aerobic exercise. Numerous other studies have shown that yoga helps with high blood pressure, depression, stress, lower back pain and osteoarthritis. It develops balance, eases tension and keeps you flexible, so it is ideal for people of all shapes, sizes, ages and fitness levels.

Yoga develops your inner strength, particularly your emotional resilience and equilibrium, just as much as your physical flexibility. It isn't just about stretching and holding a pose, it's about staying in an unaccustomed position or learning to be in a difficult place. When you are first starting, most *asanas* (yoga postures) will be unfamiliar. Apply this to your life – to relationships or work, say – and it becomes a profound learning process. In yoga, you learn how to breathe through discomfort, how to be patient and hold on, how to shift your weight to make things work.

Sitting and meditating, noticing itches or twinges: can you live with it – and, if not, what can you do to overcome it? How does your mind react when your body is trying to do something difficult? In yoga you learn to find your balance and lose it and have to find it again. You may wobble or fall, but you don't give up. Yoga is a process of trusting and adjusting your mind and body and these benefits will extend into your mental resilience and emotional wellbeing.

Crucially, yoga is not individually competitive; it's not about being the fastest or the best. Admittedly, there is a lot of 'show-offy' yoga on social media – we've all seen the athleisure-clad models executing complicated poses in stunning settings – but there's far more to it than that. Yoga is introspective in a positive sense and a powerful counterbalance to the gym narcissism that can be found online. Forget Instagramming your *padmasana* position against the perfect sunset or flaunting your flawless mountain pose on Twitter. When practised with authenticity, yoga is about 'you' working with 'you' to improve your own wellbeing. It's about finding peace within, rather than comparing yourself with the world outside.

If you have been locked into a punishing exercise regime, yoga can provide an excellent way back to a kinder relationship with your own body. There are many different types of yoga, some dynamic and physically challenging, others more focused on spirituality, relaxation or breath work. Here is a brief outline.

- **Iyengar** This focuses on correct alignment, using props such as blocks, straps and cushions. It is ideal for beginners and those doing yoga for physical therapy or in rehabilitation from injury.
- **Hatha** Strictly speaking, hatha is a general category that includes most yoga styles, postures and breathing exercises. It generally refers to a gentler, slower class suitable for beginners or students who prefer a more relaxed style.
- **Vinyasa** This is a flowing form of yoga that connects one movement to another in a fluid progression. Challenge levels vary, but it may be more suited to intermediate or advanced practitioners.
- **Ashtanga** Also known as 'power yoga', ashtanga is physically demanding. It is best suited to more advanced yoga practitioners or those looking to push their body.
- **Bikram** Called 'hot yoga', this is designed around a sequence of 26 yoga poses to stretch and strengthen the muscles as well as compress and 'rinse' the body's organs. Bikram is practised in a heated studio – sometimes up to 41 °C (105 °F) – to release the toxins.
- **Kundalini** This focuses on releasing energy in the spine and core area. It also incorporates meditation, chanting and breath work.

If you are a beginner, try out a few different classes first. Find a yoga instructor you like and explain what you are looking for and ask the instructor's advice on which form is most suitable for you.

Your workout your way

How, when and where you exercise, whether with others or alone, in all weathers or in a warm studio, and your mood – these differ for every one of us. Like food, exercise is a matter of personal preference: you might get a buzz from the music and ambience of a spinning class or enjoy the solitude of a long run alone. You might feel self-conscious in a dance studio, but love dancing alone or hate cycling in the rain and prefer to use static bikes instead. I find my early morning swim is a great way to switch off completely from smartphone, emails and social media and get some headspace. It's my quiet, aquatic time to disconnect and sets me up for the day. You might prefer a hard weights session in the gym in your lunchbreak or a sociable Salsa class with others after work. Whatever works for you, work it!

Whatever your size and shape, whatever your lifestyle, temperament and health, the opportunities for physical activity are limitless – and, as the saying goes, every little helps. Exercise benefits your wellbeing in every way, strengthening your cardiovascular and immune systems, increasing your energy levels and boosting your mood.

Ignore the fitness frenzy and listen to your body. Moderation is important, as with food, as with work, as with any other regular routine. Reframe your mental attitude to exercise: instead of punishing and flogging yourself, why not try appreciating yourself? Enjoy what your body can do – instead of finding fault with how it looks – and build on that. There is a beautiful quote from the famous teacher Tsongkhapa in the Buddhist Centre where I do my yoga and meditation: 'The human body, at peace with itself, is more precious than the rarest gem.'

That 'peace' can sometimes feel very far away but it needn't be. Strengthen and celebrate yourself instead of trying to shrink or starve yourself. Step off the weight loss bandwagon and set yourself new goals that will actually make you happy.

Relationships

Without friends the world is but a wilderness.

Francis Bacon, English philosopher

Why relationships matter

For all our recent advances in science, artificial intelligence and virtual reality, being with another person is still the most powerful experience of our lives. Think of a mother holding her baby for the first time, sitting by the bedside of a dying parent, reuniting with a lover after time apart or just a hug from a friend. There are so many ways in which relationships matter – to our brains and bodies, our heads and our hearts. Despite all the technological developments, deep down we know that nothing replaces flesh and blood contact, human company and physical intimacy.

Whether it is someone to talk to by the coffee machine, to go to the gym with, cook and eat with, shop or share childcare with, meet for coffee or lunch or just text a funny photo to as you go about your day, our friends, colleagues, family and partners come in and out of our lives in different ways. If we try living for a few weeks or even days without any social contact, we will soon find ourselves in that 'wilderness'. The connections we form with others are unique and are fundamental to what it means to be human.

This is why our relationships with others are essential to our well-being. Research shows that those with strong social bonds live longer, healthier and happier lives. Friends lift our spirits, keep us active and help us out when we are depressed, anxious or in need. A good friend will not only listen and empathize, but also help us gain perspective on our troubles. They stop us when we are losing the plot, offering wise advice and sometimes gently constructive criticism.

Our brains benefit from social contact too: friendly interactions with others have been shown to trigger the release of the hormone oxytocin. This powerful neurotransmitter promotes human bonding and sexual attraction, creating strong feelings of trust, empathy and generosity. When we hug or kiss someone, oxytocin levels increase – hence it's known as 'the love hormone'. Oxytocin is greatly stimulated during sex, birth and breastfeeding and plays a role in all pair and social bonding. It is also an antidote to depressive feelings. Other happy hormones such as serotonin and dopamine are also stimulated when we hang out with friends!

Relationships are fundamental not only to our emotional wellbeing but also to our physical wellbeing. Interaction with others promotes resilience and longevity. A lack of regular human contact can be as detrimental to health as smoking 15 cigarettes a day. Social networks and friendships have been shown to reduce the risk of developing heart disease, help with recovery from illness and extend life expectancy. Conversely, prolonged isolation can lead to mental illness and even suicide.

In the twenty-first century, our lives are scattered all over the place. We move around easily, leaving our home towns for college or university, upping sticks for work and relationships, even relocating to different continents. Our situations are constantly changing, as are the people around us. And while it is easier than ever to stay in touch with old friends, we still make new ones. Wherever we go we seek to form connections with strangers and we usually find ourselves part of new work and friendship networks. Without laying down these social roots modern life would be a stressful, lonely business.

In 2018, the Campaign to End Loneliness published findings from a range of researchers that highlighted the importance of social relationships and the effect of loneliness on physical and mental health. Their key findings included the following.

With regard to physical health:

- loneliness increases the likelihood of mortality by 26 per cent;
- the effect of loneliness and isolation on mortality is comparable to the impact of risk factors such as obesity and smoking;
- loneliness is associated with an increased risk of developing coronary heart disease and stroke;
- loneliness increases the risk of high blood pressure;
- lonely individuals are also at an increased risk of the onset of disability.

For mental health:

- loneliness puts individuals at greater risk of cognitive decline;
- lonely people have a 64 per cent increased chance of developing dementia;
- lonely individuals are more prone to depression;
- loneliness and low social interaction are predictive of suicide in older age.

The majority of loneliness research has been focused on older people, for understandable reasons. With increasing life expectancy, more than half of all those over the age of 75 now live alone. Age UK reports that half a million older people go at least five or six days a week without seeing or speaking to anyone at all, and around two fifths of all older people (about 3.9 million) say that the television is their main company.

Loneliness is not just a problem for the elderly, however. People of all ages can experience the feeling of having no one to turn to. Whether we are at university, leading a busy career, married or parenting, no matter how many 'friends' we have on social media, we can be surrounded by others and still feel very alone.

A study by the Co-op and the British Red Cross revealed that over 9 million people in the UK across all adult ages say they are either always or often lonely. Action for Children found that 43 per cent of 17–25-year-olds who used their service had experienced problems with loneliness. Less than half said they felt loved.

Only the lonely

Loneliness can be painful, but it's not abnormal. You may be lonely, but that does not mean you are unlovable or unworthy of friendship and – as the survey findings above show – there are many others experiencing similar feelings. Just recognizing this fact can help you feel less isolated.

If you feel lonely, don't give up: there are ways to forge closer bonds and find the social contact that we all need. The first step is honesty, with yourself and others. Many of us use social media to portray fictional happy lives, but this is often a façade. If you are forever putting on a front, giving the impression that you are wildly busy and successful, don't be surprised when people assume you are. There is no need to broadcast your loneliness to the whole world, but try opening up to those you trust – you'll be surprised how many others feel the same way.

Next, make a plan. Don't wallow in loneliness: instead be firm with yourself about tackling it. It's too easy to end up watching Netflix alone every night or just messing around in cyberspace. Instead of hiding behind your online profile or connecting with others from behind your digital devices, get out into the real world. Set yourself a target of attending one social event every weekend, say, or trying a couple of different activities a week. However scary or awkward it feels at first, the effort of meeting new people always pays off.

If you don't know where to start, join a meet-up. Thousands of people all over the UK make contact online and then get together face to face, through anything from book groups to yoga to wine tasting to star gazing. Whatever your particular interest, you're guaranteed to find like-minded people out there.

Being realistic

Social interaction is rewarding, but it's also complicated. With close friendships and relationships come expectations and obligations. There is no such thing as a perfect friendship or relationship: most people let you down occasionally, just as you let them down. It's worth thinking about your own expectations. Are you setting standards for yourself and others that are just too high? Ask yourself, would you prefer to be alone in perfect isolation or be close to others, warts and all? Interaction with others can be tedious or annoying – maybe being alone feels safer or more predictable. Relax, accept others and go with the flow. Sometimes having fun is good enough!

This is not about lowering one's standards, but being realistic about ourselves and each other. When people are leading busy lives, friendships sometimes fall by the wayside. I know that, in my own life, as close friends have started having children we have sometimes fallen out of regular contact. This applies as much to male friends as female friends, as their lives change. I remember that, when my big brother became a father, he stopped being up for nights out at the pub and simply wanted to catch up on sleep. This doesn't mean that friends don't want to see you, simply that their priorities have shifted. Routines that are easy to sustain in your carefree twenties – with regular coffees, cocktail nights or shopping trips – may be much harder as the reality of jobs, mortgages and families kicks in.

This may just be a temporary lull as you and they adjust to new circumstances. Try to be understanding and rational. Don't take offence if a friend doesn't reply to texts immediately; don't assume you're being ignored. Give them the benefit of the doubt, leave another message or pop round to see them. They may be as lonely as you or be going through a tough patch. If a friendship is strong, it's worth persevering.

As well as those strong friendships, take stock of the not-so-great friendships. As we move through our teens and twenties, our personalities and priorities inevitably change. Sometimes old friends change and grow along with us, but sometimes we grow apart. Some people are positive influences in our lives and worth making time for, but others are not. Do the people you spend time with make you feel good or bad? You can't choose your relatives or colleagues, but you can choose your friends! If someone exerts a negative influence on your life, it's time to step away. Life can be hard enough without toxic friends making it harder. You don't need to think that hard to recognize toxic friends: who brings light and fun into your life, who throws a negative shadow?

As we saw in Chapter 4, Social media and wellbeing, the same rule applies to online friends. You need to be ruthless with the messages you are allowing into your headspace. It's not helpful or inspiring to be bombarded daily with someone else's perfect #healthyliving photos or bragging posts. If anyone you follow makes you feel anxious, annoyed or inadequate, simple unfollow or mute them.

Above all, remember that occasional blips in friendships, let-downs or arguments are completely normal. These are part of the ups and downs of human interaction. Stick with the real people, think about what they are going through as well as what you need from them – and practise tolerance and compassion.

Loneliness too is part of the human experience, especially during our transitional years. Put down your smartphone, show some enthusiasm and be brave. There are numerous ways to get involved with others who may also be at a loose end, but you need to step forward. Whether it's a university, work or social event, don't lurk on the sidelines. Shyness can be mistaken for standoffishness; after all, no one will know you want to take part unless you speak up. Volunteer to help out with a college event, the office party or the book group: this is the best way to start conversations and, hopefully, friendships. Being brave, being honest and being out there are the first steps to forging genuine human connections.

The human habit

As we have seen, social isolation is not good for us, physically, cognitively or emotionally. We are social animals, evolved to gather in small groups and communities, whether that's the tribes of early civilization or the villages, towns and cities in our post-industrial world. We form families and spread those bonds of love and loyalty to our extended families. We have best friends and casual acquaintances; we get chummy with people at work. Depending on our personality, we may chat to our hairdresser, our neighbour or the guy who makes our morning cappuccino. We usually also develop intimate physical relationships with one significant other.

All these interactions are social bonds, some close and some loose. We express different aspects of our personalities in different relationships – most of us would not confide in our colleagues as we do with our mother, for example – but they are all versions of ourselves. These daily social interactions make up the fabric of our lives, defining what it means to be human, to exist alongside others.

Although we are social animals, this does not mean that we are all wildly sociable. Both introverts and extroverts need the company of others, but in different ways. It is often thought that introverts are shy and reclusive and prefer to be alone than with others, but this is not necessarily the case. Like many introverts I'm not socially shy and I truly love being with other people – but I also find them exhausting. After an intense period of continuous company, say a group holiday, conference or family visit, I need, and crave, time alone. Whereas extroverts recharge their batteries from being around other people, introverts tend to recharge from being alone. Introverts rely on human interaction as much as extroverts, although they may find it easier to talk one on one than to larger groups of friends. Both personality types benefit from strong social relationships, however.

In our fast-paced society, solitude is often frowned upon, seen as weird or even sinister. Being alone is literally antisocial! This is strange when you consider how much we value personal freedom, autonomy and individualism. The truth is, you don't need to be with other people all the time. Yes, it may appear as though everyone else is surrounded by perfect pals 24/7 having glamorous nights out – but of course they're not. When my partner is away I relish those solitary evenings home alone, eating dinner on the sofa in my pyjamas, maybe watching a boxset or ringing my mum or just pottering. Don't underestimate the profound pleasure to be found in a quiet night in.

Time alone can be deeply restorative, as can taking a break from Facebook, Twitter and the rest . . . See Chapter 4, Social media and wellbeing, for some ideas on digital detoxes, whether that is a few hours without your smartphone or a prolonged period offline. You could try a weekend course on meditation, a yoga retreat or simply a few days away on your own. Be curious, reconnect with the world around you – and embrace your own company.

With or without you

I'm not advocating that we should all become hermits – as we have seen, contact with others is good for wellbeing on many levels. But we shouldn't fear solitude. We shouldn't panic at the prospect of an empty evening or a weekend without plans. Silence, solitude and, yes, even boredom are character building! Whatever else happens in life, you're going to be with yourself, so it's worth learning to be OK with that. We should be happy with our own company before we start looking for others to distract, entertain or complete us.

Once we overcome the fear of being by ourselves, we can focus on developing meaningful friendships and relationships. We can choose to be with others because we enjoy their company, not because we dread being alone. Social interaction becomes a positive choice not an avoidance technique or time filler.

It's all very well referring to 'meaningful' relationships, but what does that actually mean? What do others value in their nearest and dearest?

    ❛ *Fun! Those friendships where you enjoy spending time together no matter what you're doing. Those friendships where you can sit in silence without feeling uncomfortable – they're golden. And I love those instant-connection relationships where you feel like you've known each other for ever or you can't remember what it was like before you met. Friends who stop feeling like friends and start feeling like family, the line begins to blur, sometimes you forget you're not actually related.* **Rachel, 28**

These days I just value hanging out together. If I'm honest I used to take my mates for granted. I always made time for boyfriends but friends came second – I didn't make the effort for them because I assumed they'd always be there. But then every time relationships with men went wrong I'd find myself crying on friends' shoulders. And you know what? They're still there. About five or six of my female friends have been, over the years, truly amazing. Through some serious ups and downs in all our lives, through living abroad, everything, we've stayed in close contact. I love texts and messages, but a hug from a friend is still the best thing ever. **Mary, 31**

The best friendships are just like this: through breakdowns and break-ups, even when we neglect them, the greatest mates stick by us.

As Mary points out, it's the personal dimension that matters. We now have Skype, FaceTime, instant messaging, video calls and numerous other ways of interacting, but humans still flock to be together. At every significant occasion, from birthdays and weddings to global summits, humans gather in groups. We pay large sums of money to attend sports events, music concerts or the theatre. We could watch those live events online, but we still value being there with others in real time sharing the real thing. The virtual experience just isn't the same.

Even picking up the phone and ringing someone – which, as we have seen, is a dying art and freaks most of us out – can be a rare but lovely treat. Try it and see. A conversation with a friend can lift the spirits in a way that a text or email does not. Hearing our friends' voices and, better yet, seeing their faces, reminds us of what makes them unique, their quirks and expressions, the way they laugh or frown, those memories and shared jokes. Close friends understand each other without needing to explain; they accept each other without judgement. We can share problems and victories, we can be bitter or bitchy, moody or cynical, despairing or broken-hearted, and somehow they don't think any the worse of us. Being with those we care about encourages us to confide in each other, to open our hearts and share our troubles. This reader, who recently moved back from the USA after a difficult break-up, captures why friendship matters.

> ❛ In the last few months, I have relied on my friends more than I ever thought I'd need to and I feel so grateful to have them in my life. They have looked after me, encouraged me, distracted me, listened to me and supported me as I moved back to the UK and painfully built a new life for myself. All I can hope is that if they ever need me, I'll be half as good to them as they have been to me. ❜ **Letty, 29**

Don't compare

Just as friendships can be tested and go through bad patches, so too can our intimate relationships. There will inevitably be tough times, periods when you and your partner cannot see eye to eye, when every discussion ends in disagreement, when you feel taken for granted, ignored or misunderstood. It happens to even the most harmonious couple: no relationship is perfect.

We often assume that everyone else has smooth, conflict-free partnerships, but remember that you are only seeing the public façade. Rows or infidelities, illness or infertility struggles, alcohol or money worries, bad habits or bad friends, the sources of conflict are endless and can afflict everyone, not just us. Many a couple has turned up at a party holding hands and smiling, despite having argued all the way there in the car! Remember, you never know what is really going on in other people's private relationships: all sorts of sadness and strife may be hidden behind closed doors.

This matters, because when we measure our own relationships against those of others, they will inevitably fall short. We know the reality of our own complicated situations, but we do not know their reality. Just as comparing ourselves with others on social media can damage our self-esteem, so comparing our own relationships with those of other couples gives us an inaccurate picture. So we start to feel inse-cure and inadequate. Or we ignore our partner's good qualities and see only their deficiencies. We get into cycles of complaining and blaming and forget what we love about them.

Focus instead on the positives. Make plans for shared activities so you have something to talk about: a film, an exhibition, a weekend away, trying a new sport. Confide your thoughts and feelings in each other. Talk, touch, try to laugh. Buy a small gift or cook dinner or write them a love letter. Make the effort with your partner as you used to. Remember the reasons why you enjoy each other's company.

Ditch the drama

When those tough times come around, hold your nerve. Paradoxically, one of the hardest things to do is . . . nothing. That's right: simply do nothing. Step away from the dramatic gesture, the smashed plates, shouting or tears, endlessly breaking up or walking out. Avoid the angry phone calls and text messages. Instead try doing nothing – or nothing melodramatic anyway. Take a quiet walk, write problems down, call a friend.

Sitting with emotional distress or discomfort is not easy. We are bombarded with relationship advice, constantly told to be proactive, to take matters into our hands, to find solutions, to fix problems. We are told this is where you should be at this stage in your life, this is what the perfect relationship should look like, this is how you should com-municate and relate to each other; as empowered twenty-first-century women we should dictate our own destiny; doing nothing is portrayed as weak and passive.

Well, not necessarily. Of course we should feel in control of our own lives, but we must also accept that events and emotions are not always within our control. Relationships are partnerships: like a dance, there are two people involved. Learning not to act – and especially not to overreact – is a valuable relationship skill.

It has taken me a long time to understand that sometimes things work themselves out. Sometimes people are tired or emotional, stressed about work, sometimes they have just had a bad day. It is not always your partner's fault: they may be full of flaws, but so is each and every one of us. Have you ever sat there after a blazing row and wondered, 'what was that even about?' Learning to do nothing after a meaningless argument can be the best way to resolve it. Doing nothing can be the most grown-up course of action. Instead of needing to be right, to gain the upper hand, you are simply letting things be. You don't always need to have the last word.

This applies to friends and family as much as it does to partners. Too often family occasions are blighted by petty squabbles about nothing. I have lost count of the number of rows we have had at family Christmasses about the best way to make gravy or roast potatoes, whether presents should be opened before or after the main meal, whether the Queen's speech is an important tradition or an outdated irrelevance – you know how these pointless quarrels can escalate. Even between relatives who love each other, things can get heated. You'll never 'win' in an argument with your siblings (trust me!) so you might as well just take a deep breath and smile.

Learning to do nothing can be a valuable skill in your professional relationships too. You may have an unreasonable colleague or boss, for example, and be unable to do anything about it. You don't get to choose the characters you share your working days with. The writer Douglas Adams sums it up like this: 'There are some people you like immediately, some whom you think you might learn to like in the fullness of time, and some that you simply want to push away from you with a sharp stick.' You may well find yourself working with the 'sharp stick' personalities. Rather than getting yourself into a state, complaining incessantly at home or making office life impossible, you may just have to accept the situation. You will not always like or respect everyone you come into contact with, but you still need to be able to work alongside them. It takes tact and a thick skin to tolerate difficult people, but it's an important ability.

Staying safe

Of course, doing nothing isn't always right. Long-term conflict or recurring rows won't go away by themselves. No one should put up with workplace bullying, physical harm or emotional manipulation of any kind. If there is a serious underlying issue with a colleague, friend or relative, you have to address it. The same goes for personal relationships: if a partner is demeaning or abusive in any way, you must leave. Violence, bullying or domestic abuse, whether physical or emotional, is never acceptable. There are many places you can seek help with recognizing and leaving an abusive relationship, and the first step is to talk to someone. (Further sources of support are available at the end of the book.)

Collective wellbeing

Strong social networks are good for our individual wellbeing and also good for us as a species. Interacting with others confers benefits but it also makes demands on us: in good relationships, there is both give and take. This is how we learn how to put other people first. Being kind is an underrated quality, but it is essential in any happy couple, family unit or friendship. We all know that kind people are usually happier and happy people are usually unselfish: selflessness seems to bring its own rewards.

Kindness is incredibly simple and does not require vast resources of time or money. Every one of us can do something kind every day. This could be the simplest gesture like offering to help a stranger with their heavy shopping or bringing coffee back for someone at work or babysitting for a friend. You could pick up a few bits of litter or offer someone your seat on the bus. You could do something more formal like volunteering with a local charity or befriending an older person. You could donate blood or sign up as an organ donor.

Scientists have shown that the simple act of smiling can trick the body into feeling happier. Your facial muscles communicate directly with your brain, boosting your mood when you simulate a smile. Smile at a stranger in the street and you will notice the same effect: it really does cheer you up. Similarly, helping others is an instant way to improve your mood. Whether you are feeling cheerful or miserable, reach out and help another human being. If you can't make life better for yourself, why not make it better for someone else?

Interacting with others increases our feel-good hormones and strengthens our shared social wellbeing. After all, if mankind hadn't cooperated with each other for thousands of years, we would never have survived. Everyone benefits when we think collectively about the family, the group, the community. We can all be a little self-centred at times, but caring for others forces us to think beyond our own egotistical wants, ambitions and hang-ups. When you strive to consider the wellbeing of those around you, you will find yourself becoming a happier, healthier person.

It's not easy . . .

We must fiercely resist the idea that true love must mean conflict-free love, that the course of true love is smooth. It's not. The course of true love is rocky and bumpy at the best of times.

These words, from the philosopher Alain de Botton, capture a fundamental truth, that human interaction is hard work. Relationships are complicated because people are complicated! Unlike in the movies, it's not all sunsets and red roses. Close contact with friends, family and partners can be difficult. It exposes our own faults and foibles, it can be challenging, exasperating, even tedious, but what's the alternative?

Professor Paul Dolan, a professor at the London School of Economics, believes that many of the things people think will bring contentment are fleeting and can actually alter their lives in a negative way: 'Most things we think will make us happy won't. We're really always happier if we are focusing on the person we are with and the thing we are doing right now.' It's a startling revelation that happiness is a simple equation, made up of the things we are doing and the people we are with, right now. Untold riches do not make us happier: numerous studies have shown that earning more money, gaining success or power, doesn't make much difference to our personal contentment.

Instead, it is strong social networks, a sense of belonging and spending time with the people we love that increase our levels of happiness. Friends, family and partners keep us connected to the world outside; they demand that we collaborate and interact and adapt and share and talk and touch. Relationships keep us mentally flexible, physically strong and emotionally intelligent.

Don't be afraid to ask for help when you need it and to offer it to those close to you. Ring the doorbell, pick up the phone, jump on that plane. Say 'Yes'. Sharing experiences with others leads to deeper relationships and greater wellbeing. As the saying goes, commit, you'll figure it out. Get involved in the lives of others and your own will be enriched.

Sleep

What could be more blissful than a really good night's sleep? You can't force it, you can't buy it – like the best things in life, it's free – but when it happens, it's priceless. When you've slept well, you feel you could take on the world and deal with unexpected challenges. Your mental and physical energy batteries are recharged and you can tackle even the most tedious tasks you've been putting off. Sleep gives us the resilience to face whatever life throws at us. But when we haven't slept, it's quite another story.

Sleep has become a modern obsession and most of us feel we are not getting enough. In the UK, the average person claims to need 7 hours 20 minutes to function at his or her best, but 70 per cent sleep less than 7 hours, while 23 per cent sleep only 4–6 hours a night. In the first decade of the twenty-first century, the diagnosis of sleep disorders jumped by 266 per cent and the number of prescriptions for sleep medication spiked by 293 per cent.

The 'always on' nature of our lives is a significant contribution to this problem: we are now sleeping less than past generations did and the quality of that sleep is also declining. Constant digital connection causes stress and burnout, making us increasingly unable to disconnect at night, suffering from a kind of hyperarousal that has been dubbed 't'wired' – being tired and wired at the same time.

Despite decades of neuroscience research into the somnolent brain, sleep is still a surprisingly perplexing aspect of human life. When you consider all the rituals and habits we have around sleep, our dreams and nightmares, the cycles of rapid eye movement, lighter and deeper phases, it's a minefield of mysterious hidden activity. And that's without going into the realm of sleepwalking, night eating and other nocturnal disorders.

Million dollar industries are devoted to the business of beds, pillows and pyjamas, light boxes, insomnia remedies and the rest. We crave sleep and struggle for it, but it remains frustratingly elusive. Should we be trying to sleep right through the night, monophasically in one big chunk, or instead approaching it as our ancestors did? They would wake regularly during the night, to keep watch for predators or tend the fire, and it didn't worry them – they simply caught up by dozing in small bursts throughout the day, as and when the urge took them.

Our expectations may be to blame. It may be the case that when we try to sleep right through the night, we are working against our bodies, against biology and against nature. Sleeping in two distinct chunks might work better for us – getting up for a snack or reading in the middle of the night – or even having daytime siestas or the much-fabled power naps at your desk. But for most of us, society has dictated that intermittent (polyphasic) short snoozes are not acceptable or possible: our lives are arranged around work, school and social timetables. We are expected to be wide awake and 'on' in daylight hours, and mostly 'off' in darkness.

Individuals vary as to how much sleep they feel they need. Whether that's ten hours or four hours, our bodies and our brains need this regular nightly shut-down (although our brains are far from switched off). When we don't get this, our health and wellbeing suffer. Before we get into the problems associated with sleeplessness, let's look at why sleep matters.

- Sleep is vital for every aspect of our brain function, including cognition, concentration and productivity. Good sleep enhances problem-solving skills and memory performance.
- Sleep improves physical and athletic performance, giving us faster speed, greater accuracy and quicker reaction times.
- Sleep is a quiescent time for cells to repair and recharge themselves.

- Sleep is a time of physical inactivity when our muscles can stop moving, recover from exertion and simply rest.
- Sleep protects against stroke, diabetes and heart disease. Good sleepers have lower levels of depression and other mental health issues and a much lower risk of suicide.
- Quality sleep is essential for metabolism, hormonal balance and a healthy weight.
- Sleep improves immune function and strengthens the body against infection and disease, even the common cold. Sleep loss is linked to cell damage, inflammation and digestive disorders.
- Good sleepers eat fewer calories and exercise more. Poor sleep is strongly correlated with higher food intake and obesity and lower motivation to exercise. Sleep deprivation interferes with levels of ghrelin and leptin, the hormones that regulate appetite.

But while our bodies are resting our brains are surprisingly active. Sleep enables the brain to process what we have encountered during the day, to sort through information and to consolidate learning. This is also essential for problem solving and creativity.

Sleep is one of the pillars of good health, as fundamental to our wellbeing as nutrition and exercise, if not more so. But what happens when it all goes wrong?

The effects of poor sleep

'When we are tired we are attacked by ideas we conquered long ago', said the philosopher Friedrich Nietzsche. And how true this is.

Not getting enough sleep affects our health at every level. As well as feeling physically weak, we become emotionally fragile. When we are sapped by lack of energy, daily life can look like a mountain. During sleepless nights, old fears and self-doubts resurface, memories and past failures rise up and the confidence we have by day seems to disappear. When we are exhausted, our logic and reason goes haywire and we find ourselves trapped in negative thinking patterns. Minor setbacks feel like major problems; we find ourselves becoming irritable with others, tearful or depressed. Insomnia has a real impact on our daily life – consider that sleep deprivation is actually used as a method of torture – and should be taken more seriously.

Being unable to sleep also exacerbates mental health issues we may already be experiencing. Anxiety and depression are worse when we are tired, as are paranoia and panic. Something about the silence and darkness of the night-time magnifies our worries. Our courage and resolve are weaker, we dwell on negative emotional events, we feel overwhelmed and worn down, unable to cope. Difficulties that we can approach rationally during daylight hours become frighteningly unmanageable at night. Because we are alone with our thoughts, we rush to the worst case scenario: a dispute at work becomes redundancy and long-term unemployment, which leads to us losing our house; a health niggle becomes a terminal illness – and it all feels too much. Without anyone to talk to, without the noise and distractions of the outside world, we get caught up in the incessant worry loop.

Not sleeping seriously affects our mood and our ability to cope with simple tasks. Studies show that even 20 minutes of sleep deprivation three days in a row can dramatically lower your IQ. Chronic sleep deprivation reduces our immunity and disrupts hormones and is linked to colds and flu, diabetes, heart disease and obesity. It affects our everyday lives, from relationships to career prospects to athletic performance, our ability to retain information, learn and concentrate, decision making, judgement, even driving technique.

Sleep is the single most important thing you can do to reset your brain and body clock and is essential to overall wellbeing.

Fitting sleep in

The problem for many of us is that sleep has become just another thing we try to jam into our already frantic schedules. Rather than winding down naturally at the end of the day, in synch with the darkness outside (as those fire-tending ancestors did), we're cocooned in artificial light, surrounded by music or TV or are online. We're out of time with nature's and our body's circadian rhythms, often overriding tiredness during the day with caffeine, carbohydrates and sugar to boost flagging energy levels. We're using our smartphones right up until bed (often in bed) and then we just expect to close our eyes and drop off. The sleep author and expert Matthew Walker draws an interesting analogy: sleep is not like a light switch that we can simply flick at the end of the day, it's more like landing a plane – in order to sleep we need to come in gradually and gently touch down.

Anxiety and sleep

As anyone who has experienced anxiety will know, it doesn't just belong to the daytime. In fact anxiety is often much worse at night-time, when you are lying quietly with no other distractions, no friends you can ring, no activities you can escape into. Night-time is the perfect time for anxiety, when it has all your attention and can really crank up its endless cycle of worry, panic and despair.

Like many of the problems associated with severe anxiety, this is a self-perpetuating cycle: the more you worry, the less you sleep and, therefore, the more anxious and sleepless you become. An exhausted brain is far less able to deal with anxiety than a well-rested one.

If you are struggling to sleep because of anxiety you should not downplay the problem – and you should feel able to ask for help. Insomnia is not the same as having the occasional 'bad night's sleep'. As we have seen, long-term insomnia affects your daily functioning, your work, study and relationships and is a major factor in depression and other mental ill health.

Short-term solutions are unfortunately of limited efficacy. Sleeping pills may offer relief for a few nights or a few weeks, but they are often habit forming or addictive and, therefore, not advisable in the long term.

Taking pills also does not tackle the underlying problem that is stopping you from sleeping. Similarly, drinking alcohol or taking illegal drugs may seem to offer immediate relief, helping you drop off, but they cause sleep to be shallow and disrupted and can damage your health.

Be aware that caffeine also has a disruptive effect on sleep: you may be drinking it throughout the day to counter your tiredness, but this will only set up another loop of sleeplessness and heightened anxiety. Caffeine also leads to stimulation of the adrenal glands and exacerbates stress. Try, if you can, to eliminate all caffeine – sadly this includes tea and some other drinks, as well as coffee and chocolate (see below for more information on caffeine).

There are plenty of sleep strategies that are simple but surprisingly effective.

Unwind gradually

Prepare for sleep by winding down and starting to relax a few hours before bedtime. Most of us lead hectic lives in the daytime, rushing around, fitting socializing or exercise into the evenings after work, catching up on emails or calls, and then we fall into bed hyper-alert and expect to flick the sleep switch. Taking a warm bath, lighting candles and reading a book is a far gentler way to prepare your body to drift off.

Write it out: stress, worries and concerns naturally surface at night when your mind and body are unoccupied. Grab a notebook, jot down your worries and set a time aside to deal with them properly the next day. Using a worry journal makes a real difference: just getting the thoughts out of your head and on to paper is a good way to break the overthinking cycle. It will also help you get anxieties in perspective. Keep a pen beside your bed and scribble down whatever's on your mind – and remember, this is for your eyes only.

While you're at it, write down a few things you're happy about or grateful for. These can be tiny moments of joy in your day, comfort, hope, anything. This is not about huge wins or mega-achievements every

day – in fact it's quite the opposite. It's about being mindful and appreciating the little things in daily life, those simple sparks of joy. Maybe the
sun came out, maybe you picked the most perfect ripe mango in the
supermarket, maybe you thought of someone you really love. Or maybe
you gave up your seat on a crowded bus to an old lady who gave you
a wonderful smile! Reminding yourself of the good in your life will
naturally improve your mood and relieve those anxieties.

Practise

Relaxation techniques are highly effective at clearing your mind and
preparing your body for sleep. There are many meditation and relaxation
apps available to download on to your phone and other free resources
online. See Chapter 3, Depression, anxiety and obsessive-compulsive
disorders, for more information on ACT and PMR, both of which are
indispensable habits for all forms of anxiety and insomnia, and page 144.

Mellow melodies

Soothing music helps to slow your breathing and heart rate and relax
your internal rhythms. It stimulates the body's parasympathetic nervous
system – a sort of built-in calming function – and reduces levels of
anxiety and arousal. Quiet music can help activate this physiological
unwinding process. Classical or choral music or Gregorian chant are
ideal for inducing ease and sleepiness.

As well as trying these techniques, you should be mindful of your
nocturnal routine, also known as sleep hygiene.

Sleep hygiene

Make sure that your bedroom is a restful haven, well ventilated and fresh.
It should not be too hot or too cold: cooler temperatures are thought to
promote sleep, so don't go overboard on the central heating. Equally, you

do not want to be cold, so have spare throws or cosy bed-socks available if you do find yourself chilly at night. Our body temperatures fluctuate throughout the night, in our monthly cycles and throughout our lives. I often start off curled up under the duvet and find myself kicking it off around 4 a.m.

Get rid of (or cover up) flashing LEDs, overly bright alarm clocks and other distracting sources of light. Keep all your charging devices out of the room, if possible. Make sure that your bed, pillows and mattress are comfortable – treat yourself to the best quality you can and change them regularly. If there's one place in your home where indulgence pays off, it's the bedroom. You want to feel content, cosy and maybe even luxuriant, as you lie down.

Insomnia and your digital habits

As well as the sleep hygiene strategies outlined above, it is essential to examine your online habits at night. Most of us have allowed our smartphones to infiltrate our bedrooms, with dire consequences for our sleep, and we need to reset those boundaries.

There is much scientific evidence on the damaging effects of technology on our nocturnal patterns. Sleep cycles are regulated by circadian rhythms, which are regulated by light and darkness. Melatonin is a hormone produced by the pineal gland in the brain and it plays a key role in making us feel sleepy. Many smartphones, laptops and televisions emit blue light, a short-wavelength light that has been found to interfere with the production of melatonin. Staring at a bright screen for two hours makes the body release 22 per cent less of this essential sleep hormone.

Electronic devices in the bedroom give our bodies and brains confusing signals, reducing the natural production of melatonin and thus interfering with our natural sleep cycles. Also avoid switching on artificial overhead lights or loud music or watching flashing/stimulating films. Keep your bedroom as quiet and dim as possible – to mimic natural night-time darkness – and don't turn on bright lights in the bathroom either.

If your anxiety is triggered or heightened by social media, a self-imposed digital curfew could be the answer. You wouldn't drink gallons of espresso late at night when struggling to sleep, so why give yourself a massive dose of social-media-fuelled-anxiety? Being online late at night overstimulates your brain at a time when it should be winding down and could also set off the anxiety loop that prevents you from sleeping. (See also Chapter 3, Depression, anxiety and obsessive-compulsive disorder.) Limiting your exposure to social media in the evenings and keeping your phone out of the bedroom will reduce your arousal levels and avoid the insomniac cycle of overthinking.

Stay regular

Tempting as it can be to lie in at weekends, especially if you are sleeping badly, this can be counterproductive. Improving your sleep is all about re-establishing those natural circadian rhythms: day, night, light, dark. Maintain a regular sleep–wake cycle. Get up and go to bed at roughly the same time every day, keeping weekdays and weekends consistent. Keeping a regular schedule will help your body clock to stabilize itself and will maintain a clear start and end to each day.

No naps

Similarly, avoid napping during the day if you are prone to insomnia. You want to build up enough tiredness – also known as sleep deficit – to feel ready for sleep when you get into bed. Napping affects your sleep–wake cycle and may take the edge off your tiredness, so avoid taking naps during the day. This is hard when you are exhausted and desperate for some sleep, but it will make a difference. You want your body to be properly tired by bedtime and taking daytime naps is thought to have a negative effect on the quality of sleep at night.

Stay calm . . .

Whether you struggle with falling asleep (sleep onset) or staying asleep (sleep maintenance), it is clear that anxiety is not a good bedfellow. Insomnia is an intensely frustrating experience. Logically, it doesn't make sense: you're feeling utterly exhausted and yet you can't do the one thing you crave, which is sleep. And broken nights tend to be empty, wasted time: most bad sleepers are not writing or painting or composing music, burning the midnight oil or filled with inspiration. Most bad sleepers are not even worrying about world peace, politics or how to save the planet. Instead, our preoccupying thoughts are pointless and boring: did I remember onions in the online delivery, what shall I wear to work tomorrow, what did my colleague mean when she made that comment . . . ?

A good sleeper will point out that none of these things matters and you should put them out of your mind. Even if you forgot to order onions, what does it matter? But insomnia and anxiety are not logical and it is not easy to think your way out of them. The fact is, if you weren't worried, you wouldn't be awake and worrying! It does help to remember a few basic facts, though.

The first is that you're not alone. Around 45 per cent of the world's population now suffer from some form of sleep trouble – that's well over 3 billion people. In the UK alone, remember that 70 per cent of people are not getting as much sleep as they feel they need. All the research shows that poor sleep is on the increase.

The second is that, although sleep disturbance isn't good for your wellbeing, it won't kill you. Even when you're lying wide awake, you're physically resting and that is beneficial for your body. Try not to add to your worries: poor sleep is serious but not life-threatening. No matter how tired you feel, you will cope with whatever the next day brings.

Basic meditation and mindfulness exercises are ideal for reducing anxiety and arousal and winding down at night. You could also try some simple thinking, breathing and muscle relaxation.

- **Detach and relax** When you feel your mind racing, don't try to control your thoughts. Instead, try to detach a little. Get some distance from your busy brain. Don't get caught up: just observe your thoughts and let them go.

- **Just breathe** Along with this mental detachment, focus on the simple act of breathing. This is an effective technique to distract yourself from overthinking. Breathe in deeply for a count of 3, hold for a short while, and exhale slowly. Then count to 20 or 50 or 100. You may even find that you've drifted off before you reach your chosen target.

- **PMR** This is another highly effective sleep technique that involves clenching each muscle tightly, holding the clench and then releasing it. Start with your toes: clench every muscle in your toes, then your feet, then your calves, clenching each as tightly and for as long as you can bear, then relax. Feel the difference between tension – when your muscles are clenched – and relaxation. Work your way slowly up the body, through your thighs, buttocks, stomach and all through your upper body. Don't leave out the muscles in your neck, your jaw and your forehead – we unconsciously hold a lot of tension in our faces. This is a miraculous exercise: by the end, every muscle in your body will be thoroughly relaxed, and you'll feel like you're floating.

There are many sleep and relaxation apps available online, some with soothing music, others that talk you through different visualization exercises.

The most important lesson to take from all this, whatever your chosen relaxation method, is to stay calm. Anxiety increases night-time arousal and traps the brain in self-perpetuating cycles of anxiety and wakefulness. Experiment with different techniques and see what works for you. With breathing, visualization and muscle relaxation, you can gently detach yourself from the cycle and just rest.

Working out

Physical activity is beneficial in preparing the mind and body for rest. Exercise triggers the release of chemicals and hormones that improve sleep quality. Late afternoon is an ideal time to exercise, although any time during the day is fine. Don't exercise too close to bedtime, as this raises the body's temperature and heart rate and stimulates adrenaline and brain activity. Above all, stay active throughout the day – when you're physically tired, you're more likely to drop off.

Food and drink

Eating well is just as important as exercise when it comes to quality sleep. A healthy balanced diet will give you enough energy to function during the day and switch off at night. Try not to eat just before bed, as this overloads your digestive system at a time when it should be slowing down – but don't go to bed hungry. There's nothing like an empty stomach to keep you awake at night.

Certain foods are known to promote the release of melatonin. Include these in your evening meal or have a sleep-inducing bedtime snack.

- Turkey and lettuce contain tryptophan, the precursor of melatonin.
- Honey contains glucose, which lowers orexin, a neurotransmitter that makes you more alert.
- Marmite, almonds and oatcakes make good night-time snacks.
- Bananas contain high levels of serotonin and magnesium.
- Camomile and warm milk are snooze-inducing bedtime drinks.

If you're hungry in the night, don't lie there with a rumbling stomach. Breakfast is probably a long way off! Get up and have something plain: a biscuit and a mug of warm milk, say, or a banana and a cup of chamomile tea.

Be aware that some foods and drinks can disrupt sleep, however. Two important substances to avoid are caffeine and alcohol.

- Caffeine is a stimulant found in many foods and drinks, and it stays in your system for hours. That afternoon pick-me-up cup of tea or coffee could well be affecting your sleep. If you are prone to insomnia, limit your caffeine consumption to the morning. If you cannot cut out coffee altogether, at least switch to decaffeinated versions after lunchtime. You could see a marked difference in your quality of sleep. Don't forget that chocolate also contains caffeine.
- Green tea is a good alternative: it contains around 23 mg of caffeine in a mug, compared with up to 150 mg in a latte. Green tea is also packed full of healthy polyphenols and antioxidants, which strengthen your immune system and protect against cancer and heart disease.
- Alcohol is another no-no. Although it relaxes you at first, it also dehydrates you and disrupts good-quality sleep. Avoid drinking excessive amounts of alcohol, especially right before bed.

Use the night-time

Sleep experts recommend getting out of bed if you are experiencing prolonged periods of insomnia: instead of lying awake, get up and change your physical environment. This is an important way to break the link between wakefulness and bed, making bedtime a less fearful experience. It can also change your mindset and distract you from the frustration of sleeplessness. Bad sleepers often find they fall asleep when they get up, do something else and then go back to bed.

If you are still awake, use the night-time productively. Map out the plot for your bestselling crime thriller, work out the business plan for your new fashion line or cosmetics range. Or just allow your mind to drift into fantasy-land. Imagine you have won the lottery. Plan that trip around the world or design your dream home. You might not be able to sleep but you can use those extra hours to develop your own ambitions. Let your mind wander and see where it takes you.

Keep an open mind. Different things may work for you in different circumstances. It can be exasperating when friends or experts recommend pillow spray or lavender oils or milky drinks – do they think you haven't tried that?! – but don't dismiss them out of hand. The more soothing and self-care you give yourself when it comes to your nightly routine the better. Give the bedtime baths and the Epsom salts a go; after all, they can't hurt.

As well as eliminating obvious sources of disturbance, be mindful of those external factors: street lights, police sirens or traffic noise. If your sleep is affected by noisy family, flatmates or partner, try ear plugs. An eye mask can be effective if you are light-sensitive, especially during the spring and summer months when the mornings are getting lighter earlier.

Your wellbeing

Insomnia is distressing but it is not a life sentence. Your disturbed sleep will not necessarily be for ever. Human life has its ups and downs and we are sensitive, emotional and irrational creatures, especially when tired! For most of us there will be phases when anxiety, stress or depression will affect our ability to wind down and drop off. This is normal and inevitable. From work to relationships to money to health, there is plenty to worry about in daily life.

But you can help yourself. You can investigate your own sleep problems: what helps, what harms? You can overhaul your sleep hygiene, making your bedroom as restful and cave-like as possible. You can – and must – set stricter boundaries about smartphones and other digital devices in the bedroom! You can try deep breathing and relaxation techniques. You can address any noise and light issues. You can examine your nutrition and exercise habits.

And don't let insomnia take over your life. Of course it's troublesome, but it shouldn't stop you from living life to the full. Pledge to do something every day that matters to you – not for your family or your friends or your boss, but simply for you – something that furthers your personal goals. Maybe half an hour learning Russian on the train or 20 minutes on the exercise bike while watching TV or writing a few hundred words of that novel. Feeling stuck and frustrated is a major source of insomnia. When you're achieving something, you'll feel mentally tired, personally content and more ready for sleep. Emotional wellbeing and sleep go hand in hand: each one will improve the other.

Final word

If I could write a wellbeing prescription for you, for me and for the modern world it would go something like this: slow down, disconnect from technology, reconnect with other human beings and nature. Eat, read, walk and sleep. Give yourself permission to rest, to laugh, to dance, sometimes to cry. Hurt if it hurts, but be brave enough to ask for help. Spend time with the people you love. Prioritize healthy nutrition, exercise, friends, family and love over social media, work and money. More reality, less virtual reality. Respect your body unconditionally (and others will too). Don't hide your scars: every one of them is part of you and your past experiences. When things get tough, stick with it; don't abandon yourself.

Theodore Roosevelt's advice, 'Do what you can, with what you have, where you are', resonates with me because it is honest. It speaks to something both realistic and brave about doing your best with yourself as you are, but also making the best of whatever and wherever that self might be. Accepting oneself while also striving for better is a good aim, I think. It is certainly relevant to this wellbeing journey.

In this book I have offered my thoughts on how we can improve our wellbeing, but our life experiences will be as varied as we are unique. I hope the experiences I have included from some wonderful women in their own words remind you that, first of all, we are all different and, second, we are not that different after all! Whatever's going on inside your head, you're not dysfunctional or weird or broken – and you're not alone. Throwing off the secrecy and shame of mental health problems is one of the most significant steps on the road to recovery. When you open up and start to speak your truth, you will find many others who understand. It's miserable to suffer in silence and it keeps us trapped. Deciding to be honest and seek help is immensely liberating.

Whether it's depression or loneliness, anxiety or eating disorders, emotional distress, physical illness or other personal setbacks, others have trodden this path before us and survived. These conditions do not define us, but they are part of life. The mental health challenges are not pleasant but they are not uncommon; ultimately, facing them makes us stronger, kinder people.

The journey towards wellbeing is part of the experience. No one else can tell you how to achieve that 'perfect' balance but the important thing is to embrace the journey with gusto. Explore, experiment and find out what works for your body and your mind.

If I had to boil it down to just three essential ingredients for our wellbeing, these are the ones I would choose.

- **Bravery** Whether it's faking it till you make it, bluffing or smiling through tears, bravery is essential for everyday life. Fear is one of the greatest barriers to happiness and personal development. Fear holds us back in so many ways: fear of making a fool of ourselves, fear of not being liked, fear of making the wrong choices, fear of drawing negative attention, fear of overreaching or overachieving, fear of being judged, fear of failure. We can't eliminate fear altogether, but we mustn't allow it to damage our confidence. Think deeply about what you are scared of, and then ask, what is the absolute worst that can happen? The fear is usually greater than the reality. Bravery means ignoring the inner self-doubt, taking a deep breath and believing in yourself. 'Leap and the net will appear.' Whatever happens, you'll be OK.

- **Resilience** Like bravery, resilience is a valuable skill for coping with whatever life throws at us. We cannot control what happens – illness or tragedy can strike at any time – but we can control how we respond. Developing a resilient inner core, like scaffolding that will hold you up when everything collapses, is essential. The strongest, happiest people are those who are flexible, adaptable and resilient. Think of trees in a storm: channel the young flexible saplings, adaptable and resilient no matter how strong the winds, instead of the brittle old oaks that break under pressure. Resilience does not mean that you become hard or unfeeling, simply that you have inner resources to draw upon. When the unexpected happens, you don't fall apart.

- **Kindness** Kindness is an underrated quality in modern life – but if you practise it, it will return to you tenfold. Don't waste your emotional energy on berating or hating yourself. Instead of self-criticism, reinvest in self-development. A little inner belief goes a long way. Kindness to yourself and others is a basic ingredient of every good friendship and relationship; it improves your outlook, your health and self-image. It will transform the way that you approach opportunities and setbacks, the way you view the past and the future, and it will benefit your wellbeing immeasurably.

Bravery, resilience and kindness: some of the qualities and attributes we can all adopt for a bit more confidence, a bit more self-esteem and a whole lot more happiness. Of course this sounds simpler than it is (and often I fail to adopt them myself), but the great thing about wellbeing is that it is truly self-defining: no one else can dictate what it means for you. It's not about the perfect body, the best academic achievements, the busiest social life or the highest salary. Wellbeing is about authenticity and being true to your own health, both mental and physical. Genuine wellbeing comes from doing what you love and loving what you do, believing in yourself however unconventional your path.

I hope I have helped you to think about what helps and harms on the lifelong journey towards better wellbeing. If you're struggling, start small. Take a look at your sleep patterns or dietary choices, consider whether you could swap punishing exercise for gentler alternatives.

Look at how social media is affecting you. Maybe you could incorporate some breathing or meditation techniques into your morning routine, or simply decide to take life at a slower pace for a few days. Less crash dieting and instant gratification, more walks in nature and slow cooking and candles. Buy yourself some indulgent chocolate or wine and savour every mouthful. Keep your eyes open to the beauty all around you. Write about your anxieties (remember the worry journal) and also write up your joys.

Find something you love and practise it – at least ten thousand times! When you find work you really enjoy, daily life won't be a slog. Reach for opportunities and believe in yourself, but keep learning, keep practising and stay open to advice, criticism and input from others.

When things get tough, focus on small daily pleasures. Appreciate your first coffee of the day or the sun on your face. Life mostly isn't about the major events, it's about existing in the here and now. Sometimes it's about getting through the next hour or day. We live so much in the past and the future, but the present moment is all we truly have.

Wellbeing comes in all shapes and sizes, as do our bodies, as do our hopes and dreams. I don't have any simple answers but I hope I have offered some suggestions that resonate with you. Perhaps this book has reminded you of where your strengths lie and all the ways in which you are unique. I hope it has sparked off some ideas for the changes you could make to your own wellbeing. And I hope you start to make those changes right away.

Further reading and resources

Further reading

Law, Graham and Pascoe, Shane (2017) *Sleep Better: The science and the myths*. London: Sheldon Press.

McGregor, Renee (2017) *Orthorexia: When good eating goes bad*. London: Nourish Books.

Maitland, Sara (2014) *How to Be Alone*. London: Macmillan.

Walker, Matthew (2017) *Why We Sleep: The new science of sleep and dreams*. London: Allen Lane.

Websites and organizations

Anxiety UK
Zion Community Centre
339 Stretford Road
Hulme
Manchester M15 4ZY
Tel.: 03444 775 774 (helpline: 9.30 a.m. to 5.30 p.m., Monday to Friday)
Website: www.anxietyuk.org.uk
A charity offering online resources, forums, live chats and email support.

Beat Eating Disorders

Unit 1

Chalk Hill House

19 Rosary Road

Norwich

Norfolk NR1 1SZ

Tel.: 0300 123 355 (adult helpline 0808 801 0677; youthline 0808 801 0711; studentline 0808 801 0811)

Website: www.beateatingdisorders.org.uk

MIND

15–19 Broadway

Stratford

London E15 4BQ

Tel.: 020 8519 2122

Website: www.mind.org.uk

The UK's leading mental health charity, providing information and support for a wide range of mental illnesses.

Triumph Over Phobia

PO Box 3760

Bath BA2 3WY

Tel.: 01225 571740

Website: www.top.org

Charity running local groups for people with anxiety, panic or obsessive-compulsive disorders.

British Association for Behavioural and Cognitive Psychotherapies

Imperial House

Hornby Street

Bury

Lancashire BL9 5BN

Tel.: 0161 705 4304

Website: www.bacp.com

The website provides information about cognitive and behavioural therapy and a list of accredited CBT practitioners.

Overcoming Common Problems Series

Selected titles

A full list of titles is available from Sheldon Press,
36 Causton Street, London SW1P 4ST and on our website at
www.sheldonpress.co.uk

Overcoming Common Problems Series

Dr Dawn's Guide to Digestive Health
Dr Dawn Harper

Dr Dawn's Guide to Healthy Eating for Diabetes
Dr Dawn Harper

Dr Dawn's Guide to Healthy Eating for IBS
Dr Dawn Harper

Dr Dawn's Guide to Heart Health
Dr Dawn Harper

Dr Dawn's Guide to Sexual Health
Dr Dawn Harper

Dr Dawn's Guide to Toddler Health
Dr Dawn Harper

Dr Dawn's Guide to Weight and Diabetes
Dr Dawn Harper

Dr Dawn's Guide to Women's Health
Dr Dawn Harper

Dr Dawn's Guide to Your Baby's First Year
Dr Dawn Harper

Dying for a Drink: All you need to know to beat the booze
Dr Tim Cantopher

The Empathy Trap: Understanding antisocial personalities
Dr Jane McGregor and Tim McGregor

Epilepsy: Complementary and alternative treatments
Dr Sallie Baxendale

Everything Your GP Doesn't Have Time to Tell You about Alzheimer's
Dr Matt Piccaver

Everything Your GP Doesn't Have Time to Tell You about Arthritis
Dr Matt Piccaver

Fibromyalgia: Your treatment guide
Christine Craggs-Hinton

The Fibromyalgia Healing Diet
Christine Craggs-Hinton

Gestational Diabetes: Your survival guide to diabetes in pregnancy
Dr Paul Grant

Hay Fever: How to beat it
Dr Paul Carson

The Heart Attack Survival Guide
Mark Greener

The Holistic Guide for Cancer Survivors
Mark Greener

The Holistic Health Handbook
Mark Greener

Hope and Healing after Stillbirth and Early Baby Loss
Professor Kevin Gournay and Dr Brenda Ashcroft

How to Eat Well When You Have Cancer
Jane Freeman

How to Lower Your Blood Presssure: And keep it down
Christine Craggs-Hinton

How to Stop Worrying
Dr Frank Tallis

IBS: Dietary advice to calm your gut
Alex Gazzola and Julie Thompson

Invisible Illness: Coping with misunderstood conditions
Megan A. Arroll

The Irritable Bowel Diet Book
Rosemary Nicol

Jealousy: Why it happens and how to overcome it
Dr Paul Hauck

Living with Angina
Dr Tom Smith

Living with Fibromyalgia
Christine Craggs-Hinton

Living with Hearing Loss
Dr Don McFerran, Lucy Handscomb and Dr Cherilee Rutherford

Living with Multiple Sclerosis
Mark Greener

Living with the Challenges of Dementia: A guide for family and friends
Patrick McCurry

Living with Tinnitus and Hyperacusis
Dr Laurence McKenna, Dr David Baguley and Dr Don McFerran

Mental Health in Children and Young People: Spotting symptoms and seeking help early
Dr Sarah Vohra

Motor Neurone Disease: A family affair
Dr David Oliver

The Multiple Sclerosis Diet Book
Tessa Buckley

Overcoming Common Problems Series

Lists of titles in the Mindful Way and Sheldon Short Guides series are also available from Sheldon Press.